My
Pages®

Gary Rosenzweig

QUE

800 East 96th Street,
Indianapolis, Indiana 46240 USA

My Pages®

Copyright © 2013 by Pearson Education, Inc.

ISBN-13: 978-07897-5007-5

ISBN-10: 0-7897-5007-4

The Library of Congress Cataloging-in-Publication Data is on file.

Printed in the United States of America

First Printing: September 2012

Trademarks

All terms mentioned in this book that are known to be trademarks or service marks have been appropriately capitalized. Que Publishing cannot attest to the accuracy of this information. Use of a term in this book should not be regarded as affecting the validity of any trademark or service mark.

Warning and Disclaimer

Every effort has been made to make this book as complete and as accurate as possible, but no warranty or fitness is implied. The information provided is on an "as is" basis. The author and the publisher shall have neither liability nor responsibility to any person or entity with respect to any loss or damages arising from the information contained in this book.

Bulk Sales

Que Publishing offers excellent discounts on this book when ordered in quantity for bulk purchases or special sales. For more information, please contact

U.S. Corporate and Government Sales

1-800-382-3419

corpsales@pearsontechgroup.com

For sales outside of the U.S., please contact

International Sales

international@pearsoned.com

Editor-in-Chief
Greg Wiegand

Acquisitions Editor
Laura Norman

Development Editor
Keith Cline

Managing Editor
Sandra Schroeder

Project Editor
Mandie Frank

Copy Editor
Bart Reed

Indexer
Larry Sweazy

Proofreader
Paula Lowell

Technical Editor
Jennifer Ackerman-Kettell

Editorial Assistant
Cindy Teeters

Designer
Anne Jones

Compositor
Tricia Bronkella

Contents at a Glance

Table of Contents

About the Author

Gary Rosenzweig is an Internet entrepreneur, software developer, and technology writer. He runs CleverMedia, Inc., which produces websites, computer games, apps, and podcasts.

CleverMedia's largest site, MacMost.com, features video tutorials for Apple enthusiasts. It includes many videos on using Macs, iPhones, and iPads.

Gary has written numerous computer books, including *ActionScript 3.0 Game Programming University*, *MacMost.com Guide to Switching to the Mac*, and *Special Edition Using Director MX*.

Gary lives in Denver, Colorado, with his wife, Debby, and daughter, Luna. He has a computer science degree from Drexel University and a master's degree in journalism from the University of North Carolina at Chapel Hill.

Website: http://garyrosenzweig.com

Twitter: http://twitter.com/rosenz

Acknowledgments

Thanks, as always, to my wife, Debby, and my daughter, Luna. Also thanks to the rest of my family: Jacqueline Rosenzweig, Jerry Rosenzweig, Larry Rosenzweig, Tara Rosenzweig, Rebecca Jacob, Barbara Shifrin, Richard Shifrin, Barbara H. Shifrin, Tage Thomsen, Andrea Thomsen, and Sami Balestri.

Thanks to all the people who watch the show and participate at the MacMost website.

Thanks to everyone at Pearson Education who worked on this book: Laura Norman, Mandie Frank, Keith Cline, Bart Reed, Sandra Schroeder, Jennifer Ackerman-Kettell, Cindy Teeters, Anne Jones, and Greg Wiegand.

We Want to Hear from You!

As the reader of this book, *you* are our most important critic and commentator. We value your opinion and want to know what we're doing right, what we could do better, what areas you'd like to see us publish in, and any other words of wisdom you're willing to pass our way.

We welcome your comments. You can email or write to let us know what you did or didn't like about this book—as well as what we can do to make our books better.

Please note that we cannot help you with technical problems related to the topic of this book.

When you write, please be sure to include this book's title and author as well as your name and email address. We will carefully review your comments and share them with the author and editors who worked on the book.

Email: feedback@quepublishing.com

Mail: Que Publishing
ATTN: Reader Feedback
800 East 96th Street
Indianapolis, IN 46240 USA

Reader Services

Visit our website and register this book at quepublishing.com/register for convenient access to any updates, downloads, or errata that might be available for this book.

Create, open, and
save documents

Creating basic
word processing
documents

Using full
screen mode

From Senet to Space War

Games predate written history. It seems that we have always been interested in building little virtual realities where we can compete.

The Evolution of Board Games

The first board games were racing games, much like today's backgammon. One of the oldest game boards in existence is for a game called Senet, which was popular in Egypt more than 2,000 years ago.

The game involved two players, each of whom had several pieces. The players threw sticks, because dice had not yet been invented, and moved their pieces along the board. The goal was to get your pieces to the end, which represented heaven.

This same game was adopted by other cultures for more than a thousand years. Each culture changed the playing pieces and what the game's goal represented, but for the most part the game was the same.

Senet's goal was actually to get your pieces to the last few spaces, which represented heaven. Many games used this as their goal. Today's game of hopscotch actually has the same goal, even though most people who play it don't know that the last space represents heaven.

In addition to racing games, another early type of game was a variety of Nine Men's Morris. This game involved a board with connected points. Each player had nine pieces and could move one piece per move along one connection to another point. If a player got three pieces in a row, they were allowed to remove one of their opponent's pieces.

This type of game evolved into games such as checkers and chess. The goal was to remove your opponent's pieces, while at the same time protecting yours.

Games like this simulated an all too common theme in human history: war. Other cultures developed games like it, such as Go in Japan.

The ultimate war game, chess, evolved out of these early simple games. It started in 6th century India, but did not adapt modern features, such as the powerful queen, until the 15th century.

Chess spread throughout the world quickly, and is seen today by many as the ultimate game: easy to learn, but hard to master. In the 20th century, the best chess players in the world are seen as celebrities, and chess tournaments make headlines.

The world of board games changed to what it is today in the late 19th century and early 20th. Companies such as Milton Bradley and Parker Brothers started inventing, mass-producing, and marketing games. New standards such as Scrabble and Monopoly were born out of old ideas. In addition, older games were codified by people such as Sir Edmund Hoyle, setting their rules in stone.

In this chapter, you'll learn how to create and work with word processing documents, including:

→ Creating a new document

→ Opening an existing document

→ Getting around in the document window

→ Saving your document

→ Using document version history

→ Using Full Screen mode

Working with Word Processing Documents

Like a Reese's Peanut Butter Cup, Pages is two great apps that go great together. It is a word processor, and it is also a page layout program. A lot of overlap exists between those two types of applications, so it makes sense that Apple has created an application that serves both functions.

When you create a new document in Pages, you start off with either a word processing document or a page layout document. If you are composing a long body of text, such as a short story, school or business report, essay, outline, article, or even a book, you want to use a word processing document. We look at page layout documents in Chapter 2, "Working with Page Layout Documents."

Creating a New Document

What happens when you first run Pages depends on which version of OS X you have. If you have OS X 10.7 Lion or older, you will go right to the Template Chooser. If you are using OS X 10.8 Mountain Lion, you will get a dialog box that allows you to open a document from your iCloud account or your local hard drive. If that is the case, simply choose File, New to go to the Template Chooser. The keyboard shortcut is ⌘-N. Or, click the New Document button at the bottom of that dialog box.

After you are at the Template Chooser, you are ready to start a new document. You must choose a template to start, even if you only want to create a completely blank and empty document.

1. The left side of the Template Chooser lists categories. Notice that categories are divided into Word Processing and Page Layout. Click the Blank category under Word Processing.

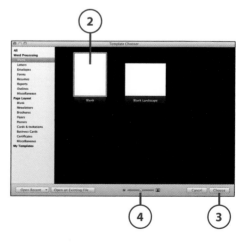

2. This narrows down the list of templates to only two: Blank and Blank Landscape. Double-click Blank to create the most common type of document: a blank 8.5-by-11-inch word processing document.

3. Alternatively, you can click the template once and then click Choose.

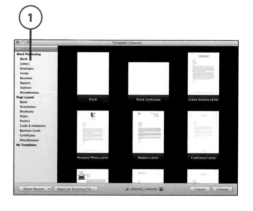

4. If you want to look more closely at the template previews, you can use the slider at the bottom of the Template Chooser to enlarge them. Likewise, you can shrink them to fit more on the screen.

Rolling Over

If the thumbnail graphic of a template isn't enough, try moving your cursor over the thumbnail. For some templates you'll get a preview of more of the pages in the template.

SKIPPING THE TEMPLATE CHOOSER

If the Template Chooser seems like an unnecessary step for you because you are always starting with the Blank template, you can set your Pages preferences to skip it. Choose Pages, Preferences to bring up the Preferences window. Go to General Preferences and then switch the For New Documents setting to Use Template. You are then asked to choose a template. From that point on, using File, New instantly creates a new document with that template, skipping the Template Chooser. You can still use File, New from Template Chooser when you want to choose another template type.

GETTING STARTED WITH ICLOUD

If you are using Mountain Lion (OS X 10.8), you can store your documents in your free Apple iCloud account instead of on your local hard drive. Think of this as a special folder that can be seen by any other Macs or iOS devices that also use the same iCloud account. So if you use an iPad with the iOS Pages app on it, you can then open up the document on your iPad. If you have two Macs, both iCloud folders will stay in sync as long as both Macs are connected to the Internet.

To use iCloud, go to your System Preferences and then to the iCloud settings. Turn on iCloud and make sure Documents & Data is checked to enable Pages to access and save documents to iCloud.

See http://www.apple.com/icloud/features/documents.html to get started with iCloud's documents features.

Opening an Existing Document

After you have created some documents in Pages, you might want to go back and continue to work on them. You can open existing documents in several different ways. You can also open documents created in other applications such as Microsoft Word.

When you launch Pages, one of several things can occur. If you were working on a document when you quit Pages, that document should reappear, as long as you have left the default Resume feature (Lion and Mountain Lion) turned on in your System Preferences.

If you were not working on a document, or closed it before quitting Pages, then you will get either the Template Chooser (Lion and earlier) or the file open dialog (Mountain Lion).

The file open dialog will look different depending on which version of OS X you have. If you are using Lion or earlier, then you will only have options to open files on your local drive. If you are using Mountain Lion, and have iCloud set up, then you will get the option to open files in iCloud as well. Let's look at that scenario.

1. Unless you are already looking at the open file dialog because you just launched Pages, choose File, Open. The keyboard shortcut is ⌘-O.

2. The open file dialog has two modes. The first is to access the documents you have stored in your iCloud account. You can switch to this mode by clicking the iCloud button.

3. The second mode is to access files on your Mac's local hard drive. Switch to this mode by clicking the On My Mac button. Then skip to step 6.

Manipulating iCloud Documents

The open file dialog can also be a way to control documents stored in your iCloud account. You can drag documents from a Finder window into iCloud, for instance. You can also secondary-click (right+click, Control+click or two-finger click) a document here and rename it or delete it. You can also drag one document onto another to create a folder containing both documents. Then you can drag other documents into that folder.

4. After you have created at least one iCloud document, you will see them appear when you try to open a file. Then you will be able to select the document you want to open.

5. Click Open to open the file.

6. If you have switched to On My Mac to access your local files, you will see a list of files in a folder on your hard drive.

7. Use the left sidebar to navigate to other locations on your hard drive.

8. Click open to open the selected file.

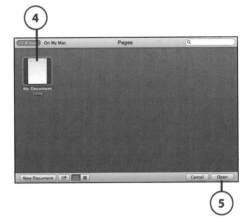

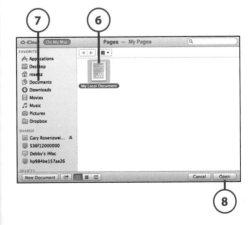

Opening from the Finder

You can also open a document using the Finder. When you double-click any Pages document, the Pages app will launch and open that document. If Pages is already open, it will open that document in an additional window.

Open Many Documents

You can open many Pages documents at the same time. Each will open in its own window. In fact, you can select several documents in the Finder and choose File, Open from the menu bar to open them all simultaneously.

With multiple documents open at the same time, you can refer to one while editing another. You can also easily copy and paste text from one document to another, just as you would copy and paste text from one part of a single document to another part of the same document.

>>>Go Further

WHAT FILE TYPES CAN PAGES OPEN?

Pages can open any current or old Pages document. So if you have a document created in an older version (say, Pages from iWork '05), it will open in the current version of Pages.

Pages can also open Microsoft Word documents. You can open either the old .doc format or the new .docx format files. Because Word and Pages are different applications with different capabilities, however, the translation might not always be perfect. You may get a window like this one that tells you what features of the document could not be imported.

Pages can also open some other file types, such as plain text files and .rtf (rich text format) files.

Getting Around in the Document Window

After you have created a new document, or opened an old one, you get a document window. This is where you do all your work. Here are some of the basic elements of the document window:

- **Toolbar:** Clicking one of the icons in the toolbar brings up more controls, such as the Media Browser or the Inspector.

- **Format bar:** The format bar contains the most commonly used text-styling and paragraph-formatting commands. It also changes to contain other controls when you have images, tables, or charts selected.

- **Ruler:** The ruler shows the margins, indents, and tab stops of the currently selected text.

- **Cursor:** This blinking vertical small line shows you where text you type will be inserted into your document.

- **Zoom amount:** Depending on your screen size and personal preferences, you may want to view your document at a different zoom level, such as 125% or 150%, for writing.

- **Statistics:** You can click here to see various statistics about your document.

- **Jump to page:** Click here to quickly move around in your document.

We take a closer look at the format bar and rulers in Chapter 4, "Styling and Formatting Text."

Changing the Document Window

You can use the View menu to customize the document window. For instance, you can choose View, Show/Hide Rulers or View, Show/Hide Format Bar.

You can also customize the toolbar by choosing View, Customize Toolbar. Then you can change the order of buttons and add new ones to perform common tasks or bring up other controls. See "Customizing the Toolbar" in Chapter 18, "Document and Writing Tools."

Saving Your Document

Before you start writing, you should save your document with a good file-name in an appropriate place in your iCloud account or on your Mac's hard drive.

1. Choose File, Save. You can also use the keyboard shortcut ⌘-S.

2. The save dialog drops down from the toolbar at the top of the document window. How it first appears depends on where you saved your previous document. In this case, it defaults to saving to your iCloud account.

3. Enter a name for your document.

4. If you want to save your document to the current location, in this case iCloud, then click Save.

5. If you want to save the file to your local hard drive, then click on the Where pop-up menu.

6. Then select any location on your hard drive, such as your Documents folder.

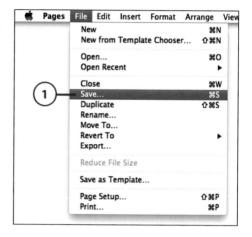

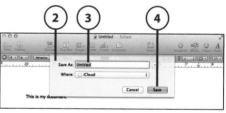

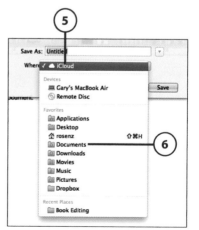

7. Click on the expansion button to expand the save dialog to include all features, such as the ability to navigate between folders.

8. Use the Finder-like interface to navigate to the folder where you want to save the document.

9. Click Save to save the document.

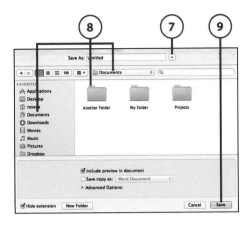

Where Should I Save My Document?

Using iCloud is a good idea for many reasons: The documents are shared between your Macs, you can also access the using Pages for iOS, and storing them on Apple's iCloud servers means they are backed up there, so a problem with your MacBook won't result in the files being lost.

But saving the files to your hard drive is better for those without constant reliable Internet access. OS X creates a user folder for each user of the computer. This is also called your Home folder. Inside that Home folder are subfolders named Movies, Pictures, Documents, and so on. You should save documents created in Pages in your Documents folder. You can create subfolders there for separate projects in any way that will help you stay organized.

You can use the Finder to create these subfolders in your Documents folder. However, the Save dialog also includes a New Folder button at the lower-left corner so that you can create new folders while saving your new Pages document.

How Do I Save As?

Earlier versions of Mac software included a Save As feature that enabled you to create a copy of your document and save it under another filename. With Mountain Lion you have three functions that replace the simple Save As command. If you simply want to rename the file, or put it in another location on your hard drive, then use the File, Rename or File, Move To commands.

However, if your goal is to create a duplicate of the file with a different name, or you are using Lion, not Mountain Lion, then use the File, Duplicate function. This creates a new document window with a copy of the document you are working on. Then use File, Save to save that document for the first time, giving it a new name.

But if you really want to use Save As, you still can. In Mountain Lion you can hold down the Option key when selecting the File menu and the Save As command will replace the Duplicate command.

It's Not All Good

The Changing File Menu

If your File menu doesn't look the same as the figures here it is because Apple has been changing it with every recent revision to OS X. So your options will depend on your OS. If you are using Snow Leopard, you will see the basic Save and Save As choices. Lion removed the Save As item and added Duplicate. Mountain Lion adds new Rename and Move To options. They all serve to enable you to save or alter the name or location of your documents in different ways.

Using Document Version History

If you are using Lion or Mountain Lion, you can save versions of your document and refer to your document history.

With versions, after you save a document, you never have to save it again. Changes made are automatically saved if you quit Pages or close the document.

However, you can still use ⌘-S to save a version of your document. Versions can be saved at any time and can be useful because you can revert to any saved version of your document.

For instance, you can save a version after completing each page of writing. After you have six pages of writing complete, you would have seven versions of your document, including the original version from when you saved before you began to write.

1. Choose File, Save. In Lion the menu item is named Save a Version, but the result is the same.

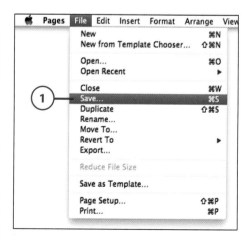

2. Type another line of text in the document and then use ⌘-S to save a version. Add a third and fourth line, saving after each.

3. Notice that the word *Edited* appears next to the filename at the top of the document window when you have made changes and haven't yet saved a version.

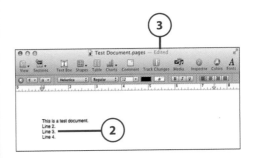

Rename and Move To

If you are using Lion, then the title bar versions menu is a little simpler, lacking the Rename, Move To, and Duplicate functions. For Mountain Lion users, these commands are the same as the ones found in the File menu.

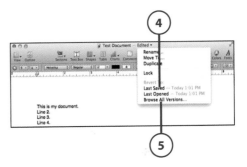

4. You can always revert to the last saved version by clicking just to the right of the word *Edited* and then choosing Revert To: Last Saved Version.

5. Choose Browse All Versions to enter a special interface where you can view past versions of the file. Alternatively, you can choose File, Revert Document in the menu bar and then click the Browse All Versions button.

6. On the left side of the page is your current version. On the right side is a stack of previous versions. Click the windows peeking out from the top to choose an old version. You can also use a special timeline interface that appears on the right side of the screen.

7. If the version on the right is the one you want to revert to, click the Restore button.

8. Otherwise, click the Done button to exit the special interface without reverting to an older version.

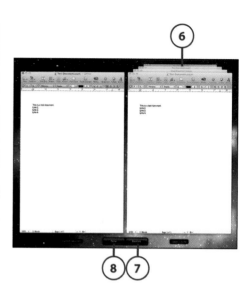

Just Want a Piece of an Old Version?

While you browse old versions, you can select text and copy it into your clipboard. Then you can exit the interface and return to editing your document. You can then paste in the text you copied. This makes it easy to grab a piece of text in an old version that you have since deleted but now want back.

Using Full Screen Mode

Sometimes when you are working on a document, it is nice to have other windows and applications around. Perhaps they contain notes or research. But sometimes it is nice to have all those other windows disappear so that you can concentrate on your writing.

Full Screen mode allows you to hide all the other applications, the desktop, and even the menu bar so that you can focus on your words.

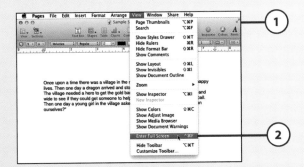

1. Click the double-arrow button at the very upper-right corner of the document window to go into Full Screen mode.

2. Alternatively, you can choose View, Enter Full Screen or use the keyboard shortcut ⌘-Control-F.

3. The document appears as a white page, and the rest of the screen is black.

4. You can still get to the menu bar, but you need to move your cursor up to the top of the screen before it is visible. All keyboard shortcuts work normally.

5. To exit Full Screen mode, click the double-arrow button, press ⌘-Control-F, or use the Esc key.

You can also see the format bar under the menu bar when you move your cursor up there, but only if your display is large enough. You can bring up and use the Inspector within Full Screen mode as well. And if you move the cursor all the way to the left, you can view thumbnails of your pages and click one to jump to it.

The Perfect Window Size

If, instead of using Full Screen mode, you just want the document window to perfectly fit the document, click the green button in the upper-left corner of the window. This resizes the window to fit an entire page exactly. If you then go to the lower-left corner and change the zoom amount, you can click the green button again to resize the window to fit the new dimensions of the page.

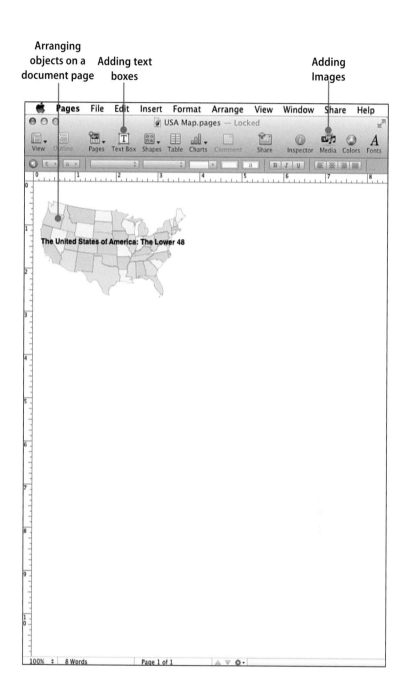

Working with Page Layout Documents

Mac users often wonder whether a good page layout program exists that they can use to create flyers, posters, and other basic documents. They are then surprised to find out that Pages can do all that and more.

Pages is actually a relatively powerful page layout application, if you know how to use it. You can use it to create anything from posters to newsletters to magazines. You can combine text, titles, graphics, and photos to design almost any document you need for work, school, or home.

Choosing a Layout Template

To start a layout document, you choose a template, just as you would with a word processing document. But this time you should choose from the categories under Page Layout in the Template Chooser.

1. Bring up the Template Chooser using File, New or ⌘-N.

2. Click Page Layout or one of the subcategories under it.

3. To start off fresh, choose the Blank Canvas template by double-clicking it.

4. The document window looks slightly different than a word processing document. One difference is the presence, by default, of page thumbnails on the left side. You can turn these on and off with View, Page Thumbnails. They can be present in word processing documents, too, if you want.

5. Also notice that there is no cursor and that you cannot click in the document area to place one or to type any text. Unlike a word processing document, there is no default location for text to go. You must create a text box first.

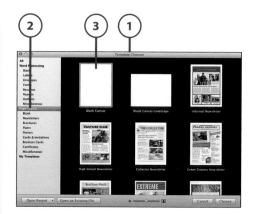

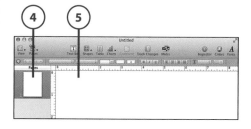

>>>Go Further

WHAT'S THE REAL DIFFERENCE?

Word processing documents and layout documents aren't really that different. Add a text box to a layout document, and it can look just like a word processing one. In word processing documents, you can still add graphics, photos, and other elements. Therefore, you can create many documents, such as reports and letters, by using either approach.

The main difference between them is that word processing documents have a large text box in the middle of each page, with text flowing automatically from one page to the next. Page layout documents can start with anything from a completely blank page to a complex design featuring various elements.

Adding Text Boxes

One of the first things you may want to do in a page layout document is to add some text. To do this, you must first create a text box.

1. After starting a blank layout document, click the Text Box button on the toolbar.

2. A text box is created in the center of the document. It contains some placeholder text. You can click in it and start typing and editing as you would a word processing document.

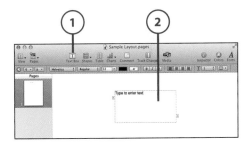

3. Click outside of the text box to deselect it.

4. Click the text box again to select it as a movable object.

5. Click and drag any of the corners or centers of the edges of the text box to change its size.

6. Click and drag from inside the text box to move it.

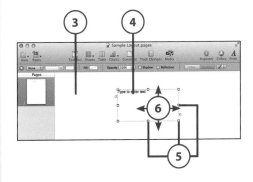

Text boxes are the main element for complex page layouts. We focus on them more in Chapter 7, "Using Text Boxes."

What About Title Boxes?

A text box can contain paragraphs of text, but it can also contain a single line or title. A title across the top of a page can be just a wide text box with a single line of large centered text. You learn more about formatting text in Chapter 4, "Styling and Formatting Text."

How About Columns?

You have two ways to create columned text in Pages. One is to partition a text box into columns. You learn about that in Chapter 5, "Document Formatting and Organization." Another is to create two or more text boxes and link them together so that the text flows from one to the other. You learn about that in Chapter 7.

Adding Images

The other major element in most page designs is images. You can add photographs from your iPhoto library or bring in clipart or other image files.

Adding Images from Your Photo Collection

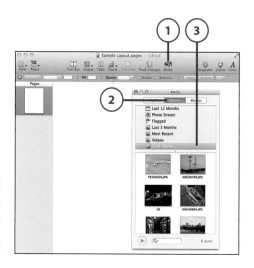

1. To learn to add an image to a document, create a blank layout document and click the Media button on the toolbar.

2. Click Photos in the Media window.

3. Select an album or smart album from the list.

4. Drag a photo from the thumbnails list to your document.

5. Drop it into the document.

6. Close the Media window.

7. Drag from the middle of the image to reposition it on the page.

8. Drag any of the boxes in the corners or middle of the sides of the image to resize it.

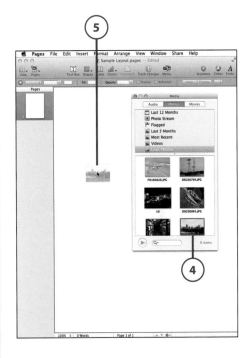

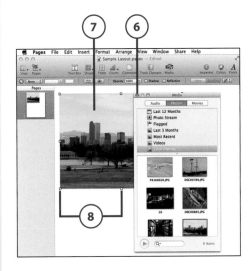

Adding Image Files

You can also add images that exist as files on your hard drive. Like with many Mac applications, this is done by simply dragging and dropping the file. You can use this functionality to drag images such as photos, or even clipart, which can come in a variety of file formats.

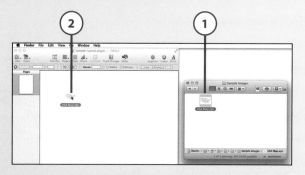

1. Locate the file in the Finder. Position the Finder window and your Pages window so that you can see them both.

2. Drag and drop the image file into your Pages document.

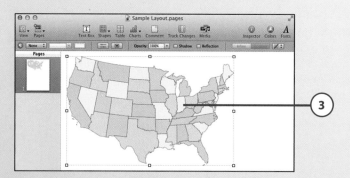

3. The image now appears in your document. You can drag it to reposition it or grab a corner or side to resize it.

   We take a more in-depth look at adding images and manipulating them in Chapter 7.

What Sort of Files?

Pages can accept many different types of image files. Photographs are usually JPEG image files. However, clipart can often be EPS vector files. These work as well as other types, such as PNG, TIFF, GIF, and more.

Creating New Pages

Layout documents aren't like word processing documents in that you can't just keep writing and they expand with more pages. You have to add each page yourself.

1. Choose Insert, Pages.

2. Choose a Text Page to add a page that includes a text box in the middle of the page.

3. Choose a Blank page to add a new page with no elements on it at all.

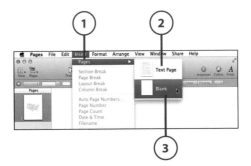

4. You'll see both pages in the Page Thumbnails list on the left. You can click either page to jump around. You can also drag and drop a page up or down in this list to rearrange the pages.

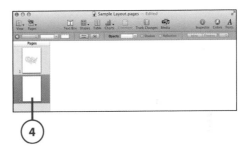

5. If you are working with another template, you may see many more choices when inserting a new page. For instance, the Informal Newsletter template gives you Cover, Photo Collage, Sidebar & 3 Notecards, 2 Column with Sidebar, Text Page, Back Page, Mailer, and Blank options.

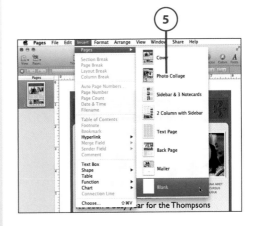

Grouping Objects

When you start moving objects around in a document, sometimes you have objects you want to stick together and then move as one. An example would be an image and title, or an image and a caption. You can do this by grouping objects.

1. Create a text box and populate it with a title.

2. Import an image and place it under the text box.

3. Select both by clicking and dragging around both objects. Alternatively, click to select the first and then Shift-click to select the second.

4. Choose Arrange, Group to group the objects together. Now when you drag them, they both move as a group. Notice the Ungroup option below in the same menu. You use it to ungroup items.

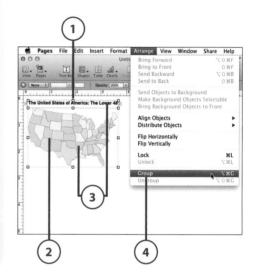

Temporary Groups

If you want to simply move two or more items together, but not group them, you can stop at step 3. Simply click and drag the items to move them as a group. Click elsewhere on the page to cancel your selection of these items.

Arranging Objects

If you have more than one item in a layout, what happens if they overlap? One item must be on top, while the other is behind it. This is true for all items on a page, even if you don't notice it because there is no overlap.

Imagine all the items on the page in a list. There is the item at the back, the next item in front of it, and so on, all the way to the item at the front.

If you need to move items in front of or behind others, you use the appropriate options in the Arrange menu.

1. Create a text box and populate it. In this figure, you can see it peeking out from behind the map.

2. Import an image and place it on top of the text field.

3. Select the text field.

4. Choose Arrange, Bring to Front.

5. The text field is now in front of the image.

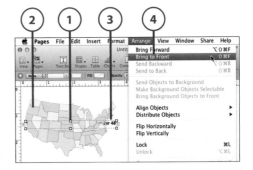

LOTS OF ARRANGEMENT OPTIONS

In this example, you could have achieved the same result by doing the opposite. Instead of selecting the text and using Bring to Front, you could have selected the image and chose Send to Back.

Also, for complete control when several objects are involved, use the Bring Forward and Send Backward options to get things in exactly the right order.

>>>Go Further

Typing special
characters

Selecting   Cut, Copy,
text   and Paste

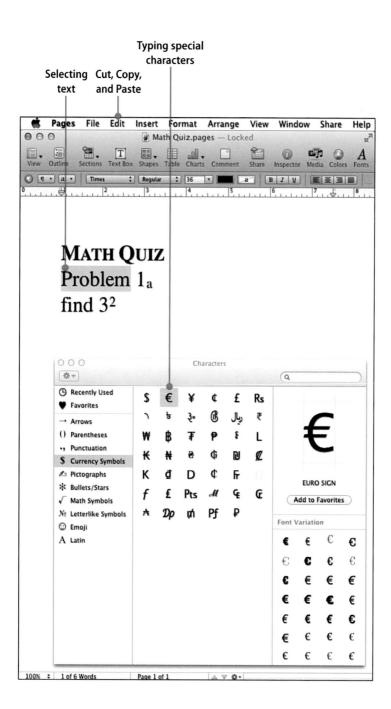

In this chapter, you'll learn how to work with the text inside your documents, including:

→ Placing and moving the cursor
→ Selecting text with the mouse cursor
→ Selecting text with the keyboard
→ Using Copy, Cut, and Paste
→ Moving text
→ Undoing changes
→ Typing accent marks
→ Typing symbols
→ Modifying characters
→ Dictating text

Typing, Selecting, and Manipulating Text

Whether you are writing a document in Pages, composing an email in Mail, or entering text into a form on the Web, you need to know how to use the mouse and cursor to select and manipulate text. Even those experienced with the basics can learn some shortcuts and time-saving techniques in this chapter.

Placing and Moving the Cursor

The cursor is your primary tool in any word processor. It shows you where the next character you type will be placed. It is also the location from which you can delete or select text.

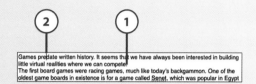

1. Create a new word processing document and type in some text.

2. Position your mouse cursor in the middle of any word and click there to place the text cursor.

Two Types of Cursors

You have a cursor that shows you the virtual location of your mouse on the screen. This usually looks like a black arrow, but depending on what is under the cursor, it can change to a hand, finger, crosshairs, and so on.

Then you have a text cursor, which is usually a blinking vertical line in the text of a Pages doements.

3. Press the right-arrow key on your keyboard. The cursor moves forward by one character in the text. You can also use the left-arrow key to move the cursor back one character.

4. Use the down-arrow key to move the cursor down one line of text. You can also use the up-arrow key to move it up one line of text.

>>>Go Further

USING ARROW KEYS TO MOVE THROUGH YOUR DOCUMENT

You can use the up-arrow and down-arrow keys, and modify any arrow key with the Option or ⌘ key, to move around in your document in different ways, as detailed in the following table.

Arrow Key Modifiers

Arrow	Modifier	Result
Left		Left one character
Left	Option	Left one word
Left	⌘	Start of line
Right		Forward one character
Right	Option	Forward one word
Right	⌘	End of line
Up		Up one line
Up	Option	Up one paragraph
Up	⌘	Start of document
Down		Down one line
Down	Option	Next paragraph
Down	⌘	End of document

Selecting Text with the Mouse Cursor

After you learn how to move the cursor, the next most important skill is learning how to select text. Once you select text, you can delete it, move it, and change its style and font attributes.

1. Click at the beginning of a word and continue to hold down the mouse or trackpad.

2. Drag to the right and release when you get to the end of the word.

3. Alternatively, you can double-click a word to select the word.

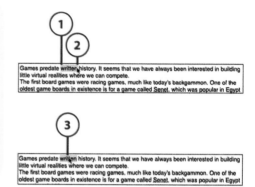

Keep It Going

If you double-click to select a word, you can continue to hold down the mouse or trackpad after that second click and then drag left or right to select multiple words.

Selecting Text with the Keyboard

You can also select text without ever having to reach for your mouse or trackpad.

1. With the text cursor anywhere in the text, hold down the Shift key.

2. While continuing to hold down the Shift key, use the right-arrow key to move the cursor forward.

3. As long as you continue to hold down the Shift key, you can move the cursor with any keyboard arrows or modifier keys to continue to grow the selection. For instance, you can press ⌘-Down to select from the cursor to the end of the document.

4. One of the things you can do with selected text is to delete it. Just press the Delete key on your keyboard to remove the selected text.

POWER USER SELECTION COMMANDS

You can also use a variety of commands and techniques to select text:

Select a Range—Click before the first character and then hold the Shift key down and click after the last character.

Select a Word—Double-click the word.

Select a Paragraph—Triple-click in the paragraph.

Select All—Edit, Select All or ⌘-A.

Extend Selection—Shift and then press an arrow key.

Multiple Selection—Make a selection and then hold down ⌘ while making another selection.

Using Copy, Cut, and Paste

The primary advantage that early word processors had over typewriters was the ability to copy, cut, and paste text throughout the document. This makes writing, revising, and editing much easier.

1. Select some text.

2. Choose Edit, Cut from the menu bar. Alternatively, you can use the common keyboard shortcut ⌘-X. This removes the text from the document and stores it in the clipboard.

The Clipboard

The clipboard, also known as the *buffer* or *copy buffer*, holds a piece of text. You use the Copy or Cut command to replace the contents of the clipboard with the text you have selected. You can also copy and cut different things in different applications: images, sounds, video clips, files, and so on.

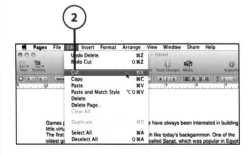

3. Position the cursor in a new location. In this example, I've also added a comma and a space at the end of the sentence to prepare for the new ending to the sentence, but you can do that afterward.

4. Choose Edit, Paste or the keyboard shortcut ⌘-V.

5. The text from the clipboard is inserted. The cursor is placed at the end of the text.

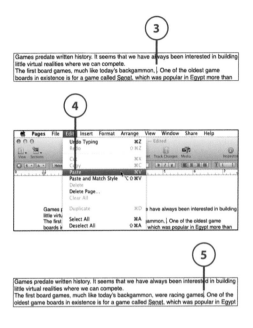

COPY VERSUS CUT

The difference between copy and cut is simple: Copy leaves the original selected text in place, whereas cut removes it. Using copy and then pressing Delete has the same result as a cut.

Then when you paste the text into place, the contents of the clipboard remain intact. Therefore, you can copy or cut something once and then paste it several times in several locations.

The clipboard only changes when you put something new in it. So when you copy or cut, the old contents of the clipboard are replaced with the new text.

Moving Text

Probably the most common way to move text around in your document is to use cut and paste. But that it is not the only way. You can also drag and drop selected text.

1. Select some text.

2. Click and hold down your mouse or trackpad to begin dragging.

3. Position the text in the new location. You'll see a light copy of the text follow the cursor as you move.

4. The text will move to the new location. It will remain selected.

Moving a Copy

You can also copy and move text the same way. Just hold down the Option key as you drag, and the text will be placed in the new location and remain in the original location as well.

Undoing Changes

Everyone makes mistakes. When you make a mistake in Pages, you get to take it back with the Undo command.

1. To undo the last action, choose Edit, Undo Typing. The keyboard shortcut is ⌘-Z.

2. The menu item changes depending on your last action. For example, if your last action was to press the Delete key, the menu item reads Undo Delete instead.

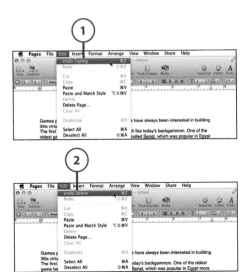

3. The undo function lets you turn back time by rolling back action after action. Therefore, once you undo the delete in step 2, you can undo the action before that by choosing Undo again.

4. You can also undo the undo. After an undo action, you can use Edit, Redo to reinstate the change you just undid.

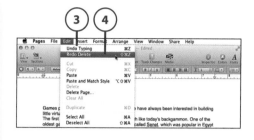

Typing Accent Marks

Not every word can be represented by the 26 letters on your keyboard. Sometimes you need an accent mark or other modification. With Pages in OS X 10.7 (Lion) or later, it is easy to type these.

1. When you get to a letter that needs an accent mark, type that letter but continue to hold down the key on your keyboard until you get a list of variations to choose from.

2. Use your mouse to click the accent mark you want to apply to the letter. Alternatively, you can press the number of the mark as shown, so your fingers never need to leave the keyboard.

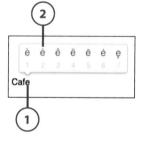

Accent Alternative

You can use the Option key to type some accent marks as well. For instance, type Option-E and then any vowel to get an acute accent (for example, á). Option-` (key right above Tab) and then any vowel gives you a grave accent mark (for example, à).

Typing Symbols

Sometimes you need to insert a special character into your text. Pages gives you easy access to the Mac OS X Characters palette, which makes inserting a special character simple.

1. Choose Edit, Special Characters.

2. Select the type of symbol.

3. Double-click the symbol to insert it into your Pages document at the position of the text cursor.

4. You can add a commonly used symbol to your list of favorites.

5. Switch to your list of favorites, which will eventually contain the symbols you like to use as you continue to add them using step 4.

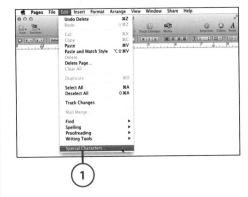

Smile!

The Characters palette contains a variety of different special symbols, characters, and dingbats. You can even insert full-color Emoji icons such as smiley faces and hearts.

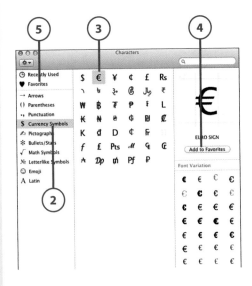

Modifying Characters

There are several ways to subtly modify regular letters and numbers. Superscript and subscript can bring them up or down compared to the characters around them. Tracking can move letters further apart. Ligatures and capitalization can change the look of words. Let's look at an example that uses all of these.

1. Start with the sample text shown here. This simple example will give you a chance to try out almost all character modifications.

2. Select the 2. The question is supposed to ask for 3 squared, not 32.

3. Choose, Format, Font, Baseline, Superscript.

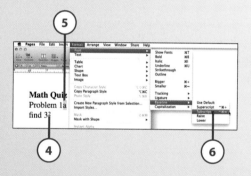

4. The number 2 is now a superscript, making it smaller and higher.

5. Select the letter *a*.

6. Choose Format, Font, Baseline, Subscript.

7. The letter *a* is now a subscript, appearing smaller and below the baseline.

8. Choose the letters *fi* at the beginning of the word *find*. Notice how those two letters merge into one character. This is called a ligature. In some cases, like in this math quiz, you may find it distracting.

9. Choose Format, Font, Ligature, Use None.

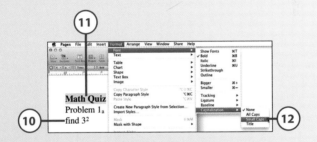

10. The two letters *f* and *i* now appear as regular separate characters.

11. Select the title Math Quiz. In addition to its being bold, let's make that text stand out even more without using a different font.

12. Choose Format, Font, Capitalization, Small Caps.

What Are Ligatures?

Ligatures are combinations of two letters into one character. Historically, they come from early handwritten manuscripts and typesetting. Pages and other word processors create these ligatures for you without your having to do anything. It is automatic and is usually desirable.

There is also a universal setting for ligatures in the Document inspector. You can turn off ligatures completely by unchecking this option.

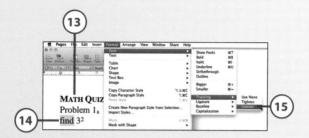

13. Small Caps is a text modification where all letters are capitals, but the real capital letters are larger than the others.

14. Select the word *find*. With ligatures removed, it looks a little cramped. Let's loosen the spacing between the letters.

15. Choose Format, Font, Tracking, Loosen. This will space the letters farther apart.

It's Not All Good

Capitalization Options

It is important to realize that using Font, Format, Capitalization doesn't change the actual characters that you have typed. Therefore, if you choose Font, Format, Capitalization, Title for the words "Hello world," you will see "Hello World." But the *w* is still remembered by Pages as a lowercase letter. So changing it back to None will set the *w* back to lowercase, and the *H* will remain uppercase because it was originally typed that way. This is one good reason to use these capitalization options instead of retyping the words. For instance, you can try a headline as All Caps without retyping it, and then switch back to None if you don't like the result.

Dictating Text

If you are using OS X 10.8, Mountain Lion, then you can turn on Mountain Lion's dictation feature and speak instead of typing.

Turn On Dictation

Before you can use the dictation feature, make sure it is turned on in your System Preferences, Dictation & Speech settings. Switch Dictation to "on" and choose a keyboard shortcut. The default shortcut is to press the "fn" key twice. If you change it to something else, then be sure to use that shortcut in step 2 instead.

1. Create a new word processing document and place the cursor in the document as if you were about to type.

2. Choose Edit, Start Dictation. Or, use the keyboard shortcut, the default being to press the "fn" key twice.

3. Speak steadily and clearly. No need to put your mouth close to the microphone. But it does help if the room is quiet with no other sounds than your voice.

4. Click the Done button to stop. You can also press the "fn" key once to stop. To cancel instead, press any other key such as the spacebar.

5. Re-read your dictated text carefully. Dictation isn't perfect and results will vary. Use your keyboard and cursor to correct any mistakes.

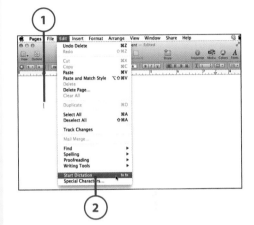

Need to Be Connected

The OS X dictation feature requires that you are connected to the Internet. The audio is actually sent to Apple's servers and the text is returned. This means that all of the processing (heavy lifting) is performed by Apple's computers and not your own.

>>>Go Further

DICTATION SPECIAL COMMANDS

While dictating you can add punctuation and symbols by speaking them.
Here is a list of some of the special instructions that dictation understands.

Period	.
Comma	,
Dash	-
New line	Return
New paragraph	Two returns
Quote	"
Exclamation point	!
Question mark	?
Ampersand	&
Asterisk	*
Open parenthesis	(
Close parenthesis	)
Percent	%
Dollar sign	$
At sign	@
Forward slash	/
Back slash	\

Note that dictation in OS X is similar to dictation in iOS, but it does not
support some of the more sophisticated commands like "No caps on." It is
possible that future updates to the OS X dictation feature could add those
commands and possibly much more.

Selecting font face
and style

Text alignment

The Australian Wombat

The Wombat is an Australian marsupial with a short stubby tail. They are found in southeastern Australia and Tasmania. They have powerful claws and teeth which they use to burrow.

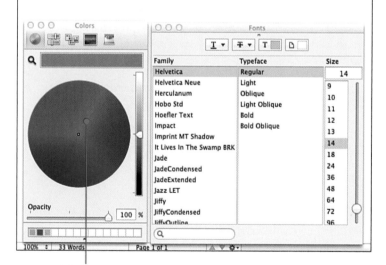

Coloring text

In this chapter, you'll learn how to change the appearance of text in your documents, including:

→ The format bar and the Inspector window

→ Selecting a font

→ Styling text

→ Changing the font size

→ Coloring text

→ Other text attributes

→ Text alignment

→ Indenting paragraphs

→ Increasing line and paragraph spacing

→ Adding tab stops

4

Styling and Formatting Text

One of the most basic skills you need to learn to use any word processor is how to change the look of text. You can choose different fonts, styles (such as bold or italic), colors, line spacing, and much more.

The key to making these changes in your document is learning to use the format bar. However, some adjustments will require that you use the Inspector.

The Format Bar and the Inspector Window

The format bar appears near the top of any document window in Pages. It contains a number of buttons and controls that affect the selected text. For instance, you can apply a style or change the font size.

You can show or hide the format bar by choosing View, Show/Hide Format Bar in the menu bar (⌘-Shift-R is the keyboard shortcut for showing or hiding the format bar).

The Inspector is a separate window. The controls in it change depending on which tab you select at the top. You can think of it as a number of inspectors all rolled into one window. The tab that looks like the letter *T* will show the Text inspector. The first tab brings up the Document inspector.

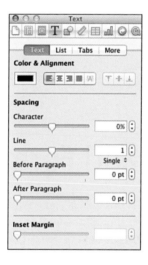

In addition, each inspector has a variety of subcategories. The Text inspector can show controls in four categories: Text, List, Tabs, and More.

In this chapter, you get to use both the format bar and the Inspector. Play around with the controls in each to see what else you can do as you follow along with the examples.

Selecting a Font

Your Mac comes with dozens of different fonts. You can use a single font for your entire document or mix several fonts throughout. Here's how to change the font of a selection of text.

1. If your format bar is not already present, choose View, Show Format Bar to bring it up. If this menu item reads Hide Format Bar, it means your format bar is already visible.

2. Select some text in your document.

3. Click the font pull-down menu on the format bar.

4. Scroll up and down to view all of your font choices. If you scroll to the top of this list, you should see your most commonly chosen fonts.

5. Click to select a font.

6. The selected text changes to use this font.

Jump to Your Font

The list of fonts is long, but you can find one quickly using the keyboard. After you bring up the pop-up menu of fonts, start typing the font's name. For instance, pressing **T** takes you to the first font that starts with the letter *T*. Typing **tre** takes you to the first font that starts with those three letters.

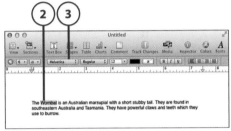

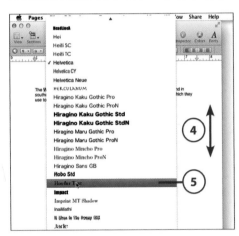

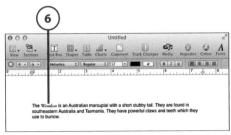

CAN I GET MORE FONTS?

You can find and purchase more fonts on the Internet. Almost all fonts you find will work on your Mac in Pages, but try to use TrueType (.ttf) files when you can. Downloading a font to your Mac and double-clicking the font file will allow you to install it on your Mac using the Font Book utility.

You can search for "fonts" in the Mac App Store and find several collections you can buy, sometimes for as little as a dollar for a whole collection. Many clipart sites also provide fonts.

Styling Text

When you think about styling text, you usually think of bold and italic. However, you may have many more options available, depending on the font. For instance, the font Verdana can be plain, bold, italic, or bold italic. But the font Helvetica can also be light, in addition to bold and oblique (another name for italic).

1. Select some text.

2. Click the style typeface pull-down menu.

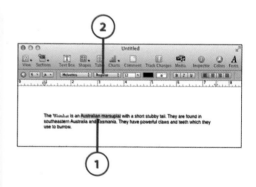

3. Select a style from the list.

4. Alternatively, you can use the Bold button on the toolbar to quickly bold the text. The keyboard shortcut ⌘-B works, too. Click it again to remove the bolding.

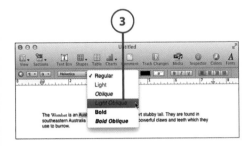

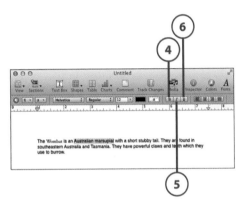

5. Use the Italic button or ⌘-I to quickly change the style to italic. You can use this in combination with the Bold button to get bold and italic.

6. Click the Underline button to underline the selected text (⌘-U is the keyboard shortcut).

What Is Italic?

Technically, an italic version of a font is a different font with a more calligraphy-like appearance, but still similar in style to the original. But often today it is just a slanted version of the same font, which would be more accurately described as "oblique."

Changing the Font Size

To change the size of text, select the text and then use the toolbar to set the size to a specific number.

1. Select some text.

2. Click the drop-down arrow on the right side of the font size selection pull-down menu.

3. Choose from the list of common sizes.

4. Alternatively, you can use ⌘-+ (plus) to increase the font size of selected text. Use ⌘-- (minus) to decrease the font size.

5. You can also click in the left side of the font size selection field and edit the number to enter a specific font size.

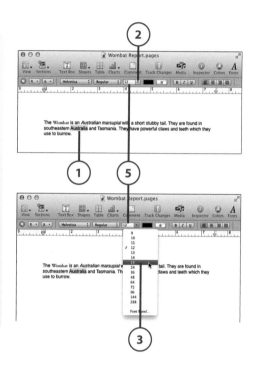

Coloring Text

With color printers more popular than black-and-white printers today, and many documents being sent around as PDF files, you may want to color up your text. You can do this by selecting text and then using the toolbar or opening the Colors window.

1. Select some text.

2. Click the text color control on the format bar.

3. Select the color.

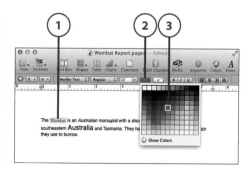

4. Alternatively, you can click the Colors button on the toolbar.

5. Select a color in the color wheel interface in the Colors window.

6. You can also adjust the color wheel brightness by dragging the indicator in the brightness meter on the right.

7. There are several other ways to select colors in the Colors window, including using meters and color chips as well as choosing from a palette and from a crayon-like interface.

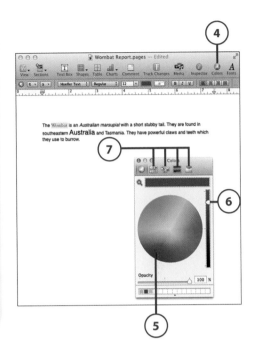

Applying Other Text Attributes

Type, style, size, and color are the basics you can set for your text. But there are other ways to style your text, as well.

1. Select some text.

2. Choose Format, Font, Strikethrough to put a line through the center of your text.

Why Strikethrough?

Although revision tools (see Chapter 17, "Reviewing Documents") make it unnecessary for you to use strikethrough for editing, you can use it when you intentionally want to show that a word has been removed in your final text, usually to emphasize a point. An example is this: You ~~sometimes~~ always want to check your sources.

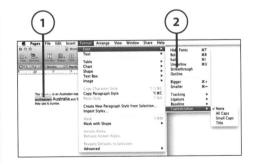

3. Choose Format, Font, Outline to convert the text to appear as outlined. This is more of a novelty effect commonly used in the early days of word processing for emphasis.

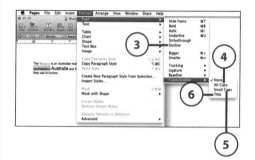

4. Choose Format, Font, Capitalization, All Caps to make your text appear in all capital letters. This is better than simply typing in all uppercase because the text retains the information about which letters are uppercase and which are lowercase, so you can change your mind later and turn this effect off without needing to retype the text.

5. Choose Format, Font, Capitalization, Small Caps. This special effect puts all the letters in uppercase, but the capital letters appear larger than the lowercase ones.

6. Choose Format, Font, Capitalization, Title. This capitalizes all the words while retaining the original case information for each letter. Therefore, you can turn this off to restore the original case of each letter like you can with All Caps.

Aligning Text

You can center text, justify it, or align it left or right using the format bar.

1. Click to place your cursor in some text. You don't have to select the text of a paragraph to set the alignment for the whole paragraph. You just need to have the cursor somewhere in the paragraph.

2. Click the left alignment button to align all the text to the left.

3. Click the center alignment button to center all the lines of text in the paragraph.

4. Click the right alignment button to align all the text in the paragraph against the right margin.

5. Click the Justify text button to justify the text of each line. When you do this, space is added between each word so that text on each side aligns perfectly with the left and right margins. Naturally, the last line of text in a paragraph will always be justified left or right.

Aligning More Than One Paragraph

To set the alignment for a single paragraph, all you need to do is make sure the cursor is somewhere in that paragraph. To set the alignment for multiple paragraphs, simply select all those paragraphs and then set the alignment.

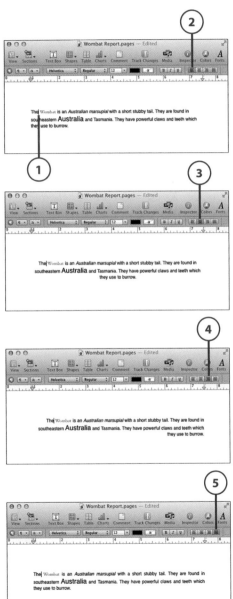

Indenting Paragraphs

Depending on the type of document you are writing, you may want to have the start of each paragraph indented. You can do this using the ruler at the top of the window or by entering in exact measurements using the Inspector.

1. Make sure the ruler is present by choosing View, Show Rulers. If you see Hide Rulers there instead, this means the ruler is already visible.

2. With your cursor in the paragraph you want to adjust, click and drag the indentation marker in the ruler. You'll see a vertical line showing you the exact location of the indent down the page, and the paragraph adjusts accordingly. If you have several paragraphs selected, all of them will be affected.

3. Alternatively, bring up the Inspector.

4. Choose the Text inspector.

5. Choose Tabs.

6. Set the value for the paragraph indent.

7. You can also set the left and right margins for the paragraph.

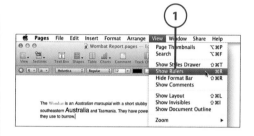

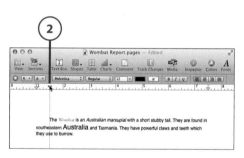

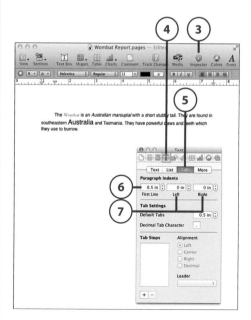

Increasing Line and Paragraph Spacing

You can increase the spacing between each line of your text, or just the spacing between paragraphs. To do this, you need to use the Inspector.

1. Select the paragraphs you want to adjust.

2. Bring up the Inspector.

3. Select the Text inspector.

4. Choose Text.

5. Use the horizontal slider to adjust the line spacing.

6. Alternatively, you can set the line spacing to a specific measurement. Set it to 2 if you want your text to be double-spaced.

7. You can also use a slider to add extra space after each paragraph.

8. You can enter in an exact measurement for extra paragraph spacing.

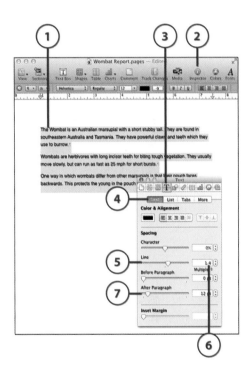

You Can Use the Format Bar, Too

If you expand your document window to the right far enough, there is enough room on the format bar for line-spacing controls. They appear just to the right of the text-alignment controls by default.

Adding Tab Stops

Tab stops allow you to mark certain horizontal positions in a paragraph so that you can align text into simple tables. In most cases, you would want to use the more modern method of tables (see "Adding a Basic Table" in Chapter 10, "Creating Tables"). However, old-fashioned tab stops can still come in handy from time to time.

1. Start by creating a simple table of information, using the Tab key to separate items in each row. If the ruler isn't visible, choose View, Show Rulers first.

2. Choose View, Show/Hide Invisibles so that you can see the inserted tabs, which are represented by small blue arrows pointing to the right.

3. Click and drag anywhere in the ruler to create a tab stop and position it. You will see a vertical line that shows you the position of the tab stop throughout the document.

4. Click and drag to create a second tab stop.

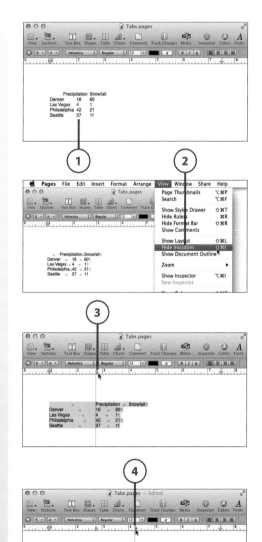

Decimal Tab Stops

A decimal tab stop aligns numbers so that the decimal points in each row line up. Thus, the decimal points in the numbers 14.2 and 7.85 will appear in the exact same horizontal position, at the location of the tab stop.

5. Control-click any tab stop to change its type.

6. Select the type of tab stop. A standard tab stop aligns text with the tab stop at the left, but you can also have text centered at the tab stop or aligned to the right.

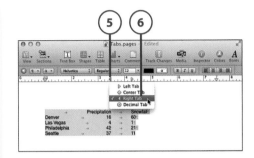

7. For finer control over tabs, bring up the Inspector.

8. Go to the Text inspector.

9. Click Tabs.

10. You can select a tab. Double-click it to enter in a number.

11. Change the type of the tab selected.

12. Add a new tab by clicking the + button in the Inspector.

13. When a tab is present in the text, but there is no tab stop, the Default Tabs setting determines the default locations of tab stops. For instance, if Default Tabs is set to 0.5 inches, a tab stop will appear at every inch and half-inch in the ruler.

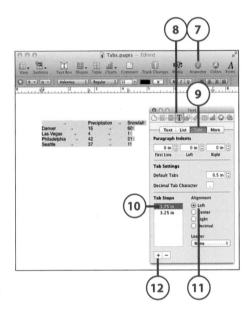

Tab Leaders

In the Tabs inspector, you will also notice a Leader setting. This automatically adds characters from the previous tab stop to the current one, such as periods or dashes.

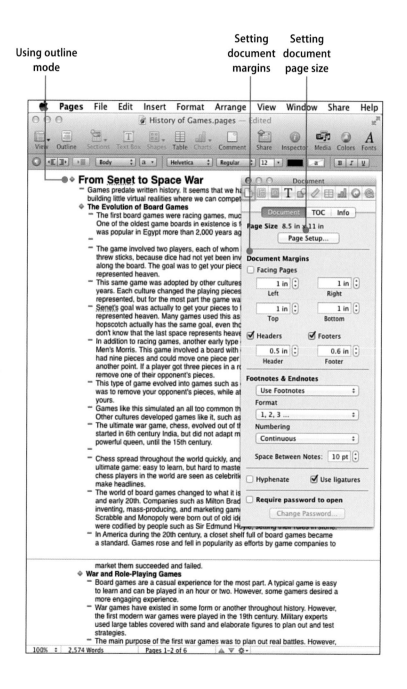

Using outline mode

Setting document margins

Setting document page size

In this chapter, you'll learn about different ways to set up your document, including:

→ Setting your document's page size
→ Modifying document margins
→ Using page thumbnails
→ Using outline mode
→ Using text columns
→ Preventing orphan lines

Document Formatting and Organization

Besides the words and paragraphs in your document, the document itself has some properties you need to think about. How big is the page? What are the margins? And so on.

Let's take a look at setting these properties as well as using page thumbnails and outline mode to help organize your document.

Setting Your Document's Page Size

Most word processing documents are created for standard 8.5-by-11-inch paper, also called letter-sized paper. And that is the default for documents in pages. However, if you want to use a different size, you can change it easily.

1. After starting your new document, choose File, Page Setup.

2. Click the Paper Size pull-down menu.

3. Select a standard paper size, such as US Legal. Notice that a yellow tooltip text appears next to each entry as you roll over it with your mouse. This tooltip tells you the standard size and margins of the paper size.

4. If you want to set your document to landscape (horizontal) rather than portrait (vertical), click the landscape button for the Orientation setting.

Custom Sizes, Too

If you don't see the paper type you want, don't worry. You can also choose Manage Custom Sizes and create a new paper type of any dimension. You can save that paper type with a name so that it will appear in the list for use in future documents.

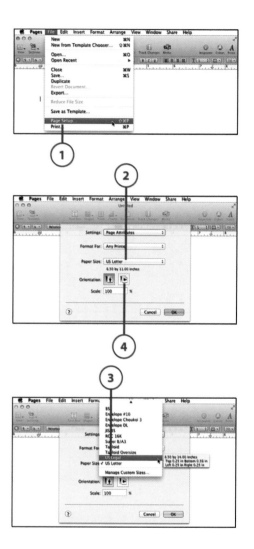

Modifying Document Margins

After you have established the paper size, you can adjust the margins (the space around the edges of the page). You may want to do this for aesthetic reasons, or simply because your printer is not able to print all the way to the edge of a page.

1. Bring up the Inspector window.

2. Switch to the Document inspector.

3. View the Document section of the Document inspector.

4. Here you can change the margins on each of the four edges of the page. Click in the fields to enter a number or use the arrows to the left of each field to change the value.

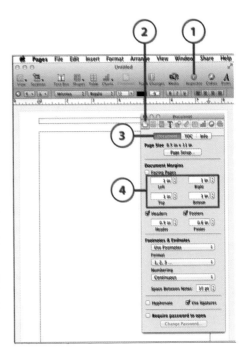

Visible Margins

The figures here show the margins and the header with lines. You can see these lines in Page if you choose View, Show Layout.

Why Inches?

If you prefer to use centimeters, or even points or picas as your measurement when adjusting margins, you can change this in your Pages, Preferences, Rulers Preferences settings.

Using Page Thumbnails

You can scroll up and down to go anywhere in your document. However, if your document gets long, then page thumbnails will help you navigate more easily. You can also use them to arrange sections in a word processing document and arrange pages in a page layout document.

Navigating Word Processing Documents

Page thumbnails can be used for the simple task of jumping from one page to the other in any kind of document.

1. Open a word processing document.

2. Turn on page thumbnails by choosing View, Page Thumbnails.

3. The thumbnails appear on the left.

4. Click any one to jump to that page in the document.

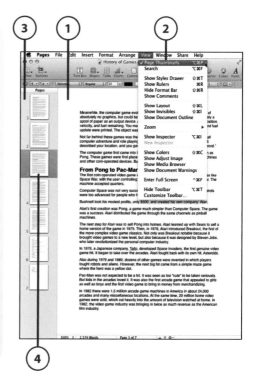

Jump to a Page Number

If you have a huge document and want to jump ahead to a specific page, you can do this by clicking at the bottom of the document window where it shows the page number. It will change to a "Go to Page" entry field. Type in a number and press Return to jump to that page.

Navigate by Searching

Another way to jump to a page in a document is to search for some text. For instance, if you know the title of a section or how a sentence starts, you can press ⌘-F, type the search term, and then press Return. You'll be quickly taken to that part of the document.

Moving Pages in Page Layout Documents

If you are creating a page layout document, each page is its own element. This means you can move pages around in your document in a way that you can't in a word processing document, where the text just flows from one page to the next.

1. Open a page layout document.

2. Choose View, Page Thumbnails.

3. The page thumbnails appear on the left.

4. When you click to select a page, a yellow border shows you which page you are on and that it can be moved as a separate element.

5. You can drag a page from one location to another in the document.

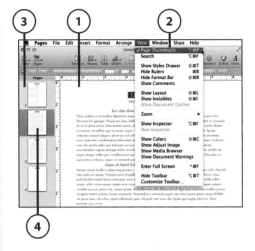

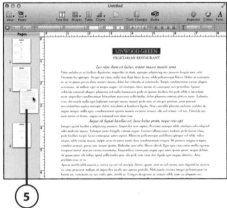

Move Multiple Pages

If you want to move a group of contiguous pages, you can select the first one and then Shift-select the last one. This selects the whole range. Now you can click and drag any of the pages to move them all as a group.

Using Outline Mode

Although you can say that the two modes for Pages documents are word processing and page layout, you could also add in a third: outline. This is really a variation on a word processing document, and can be used to create outlines as well as to help organize the paragraphs of any document.

Organizing Documents

Let's start by looking at how outline mode can help you organize a regular text document.

1. Start with a regular word processing document.

2. Choose View, Show Document Outline. You can also click on Outline in the toolbar.

3. The document now appears as an outline, with headings being used to determine the shape of the outline. Each paragraph is its own outline item.

4. You can still edit the text of each paragraph as before.

5. You can also drag the blue dash next to each paragraph to rearrange paragraphs.

6. As you drag, you can move left and right to change the indent level of any paragraph.

7. Repeat step 2 to switch back to normal mode.

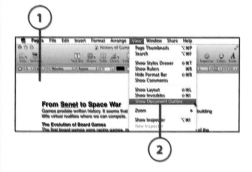

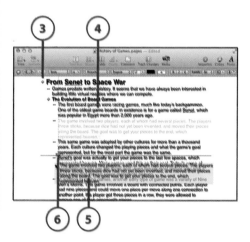

Like Using Index Cards

Remember how in school they wanted you to create a story or report by first writing everything on index cards? Then you could arrange and rearrange them to find out which order worked best? The outline mode is similar to that. You can think of each paragraph as an index card and move them all around and edit them, and then turn off outline mode when done. You can indent to group together multiple paragraphs that would normally appear on a single index card.

Creating Outlines

In addition to using outline mode to organize your document, the document could be an outline itself. If this is the case, there are some special templates that you can use.

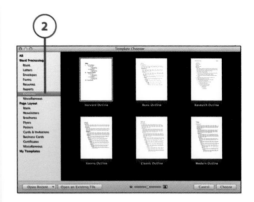

1. Choose File, New to start a new document.

2. Choose the Outlines subcategory.

3. Choose an outline template.

4. You'll start with a sample outline, complete with placeholder text.

5. Select any placeholder and type to replace it with your own text. You can click anywhere in the text to select the whole placeholder.

6. Use Tab and Shift-Tab to increase or decrease, respectively, the indentation of any item.

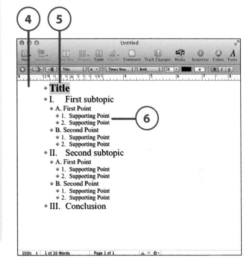

Outlines Are Lists

For more information about how to create, edit, and manipulate outlines, read over Chapter 6, "Creating Lists and Outlines." Outlines are really very similar to lists. The difference is that you are making a document in outline mode, as opposed to making a document in regular word processing mode with a list inserted as one element.

Using Text Columns

You can divide your text into multiple columns in a word processing document. You can even switch back and forth between single column and multiple columns in the same document.

1. Start with a document that contains a page worth of text.

2. Click the columns button on the toolbar.

3. Click the 2 Columns option.

4. The text is now displayed over two columns.

5. Bring up the Inspector window.

6. Switch to the Layout inspector.

7. Click Layout.

8. You can set the number of columns.

9. You can set the column width. As long as Equal Column Width is checked, changing one value changes them all.

10. You can set the size of the space between the columns.

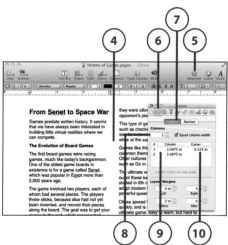

11. If want different parts of your text to have different numbers of columns, first place the text cursor where you want the number of columns to change.

12. Choose Insert, Layout Break.

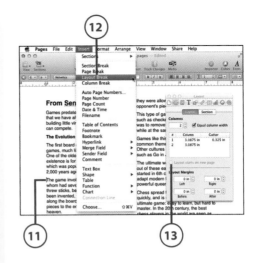

13. The Layout Starts on New Page option then becomes active. You would turn it on only if you want the next section to start on a new page. Leave it off. Notice that even though the top and the bottom of the page are both two columns, the text flows from the left column to the right column at the top of the page, and then continues to the left column to the left of the page in the second section.

14. Place the text cursor in the section of text you want to change back to a single column.

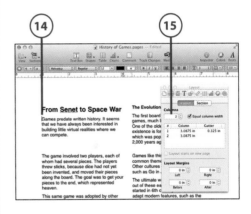

15. Change the number of columns back to 1.

16. The first part of the page now uses a single column. The second part then uses two columns. You can use Layout Breaks to create more sections like this throughout your document.

Column Breaks

You can force text to jump to the start of the next column with a column break. Just position the text cursor and choose Insert, Column Break.

Preventing Orphan Lines

When polishing your document and getting ready to print it or distribute it, you may notice that some paragraphs of text start on one page and then continue on the other. That may be fine for your particular document. But if you want to force a paragraph to remain together, or at least prevent a single line at the start of a paragraph from being widowed on the first page, or a single line at the end from being orphaned on the following page, you can do a few things.

1. Notice how this paragraph starts on one page and then continues on the other. The first line is widowed on the first page. Place your text cursor in this paragraph.

2. Bring up the Inspector window and go to the Text inspector.

3. Click More.

4. Selecting Keep Lines Together forces Pages to put the entire paragraph on the same page in your document.

5. Keep with Following Paragraph pairs the current paragraph with the next one and makes sure they are both on the same page.

6. Paragraph Starts on a New Page makes sure that the paragraph always starts a page, even if there is plenty of room for it on the previous page.

7. Prevent Widow & Orphan Lines moves the paragraph on to a new page if only one line would be widowed on the previous one, or one line would be orphaned on the next. If the paragraph is a long one, it will split it between the pages so that there isn't just one line on a page by itself. This is different from the option in step 4, which works no matter how many lines would be on the previous or next page.

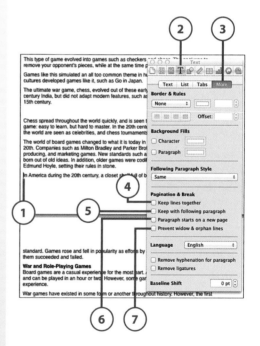

Creating lists

Customizing lists
and outlines

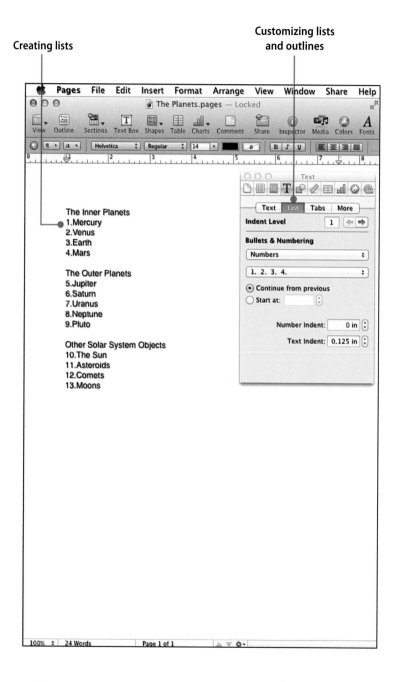

Creating Lists and Outlines

Word processing documents can be used for more than just writing prose. You can create lists of all sorts in Pages. Lists can be simple ordered items or complex outlines.

You can put a list in a word processing or page layout document. You can even have an entire document that is just a list.

Creating Bullet Lists

Lists are simply multiple lines of text that have special formatting applied to them. In fact, you can start off by just putting each item on its own line in a plain word processing document. Then you can convert those lines to a list using the format bar.

The simplest type of list is a bullet list. This just puts a bullet (usually a small circle) to the left of each item in the list.

1. Type a list of items, one on each line. The list doesn't need to be the only thing in the document. You can have other text as well.

2. Select the lines you want to convert to a bullet list.

3. Click the List Style button on the format bar.

4. Choose Bullet as the list style.

5. A bullet is placed to the left of each line in the list.

6. Place your text cursor to the right of the last item in the list.

7. Press Return, and then type a new list item. The new line becomes a part of that list.

8. If you are done creating your list, then repeat step 4 on a new line, choosing None instead of Bullet.

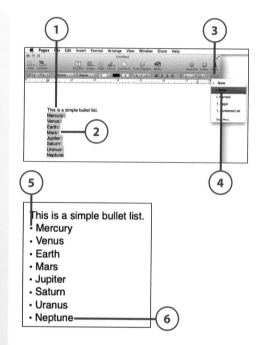

List First

Alternatively, you can click the List Style button and choose Bullet before entering any text. Then you can start typing the list.

>>>Go Further

INSERTING LIST ITEMS

In addition to being able to add items to the end of a list, you can insert a new item anywhere in the list. Just place your text cursor at the start of an item, type the new item, and press Return. Alternatively, place your text cursor at the end of an item, press Return, and then type the new item.

You can also delete items by simply selecting them and pressing Delete. Lists work just like any other set of lines in a word processing document.

Creating Numbered Lists

Numbered lists are like bullet lists in that they are just another way of formatting several lines of text. But instead of bullets, a number appears at the left side of each line.

1. Type a list of items, one item on each line. The list doesn't need to be the only thing in the document. You can have other text as well.

2. Select the lines that you want to convert to a numbered list.

3. Click the List Style button on the format bar.

4. Choose Numbered List as the list style.

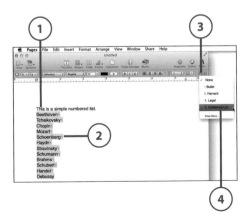

5. Numbers appear to the left of each line of the list.

6. Position the text cursor to the right of a line of text.

7. Press the Return key to start a new line and then type a new item. Notice that the new item is inserted in the list and all the numbers after that item shift to accommodate the new item.

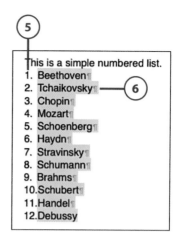

This is a simple numbered list.
1. Beethoven
2. Tchaikovsky
3. Chopin
4. Mozart
5. Schoenberg
6. Haydn
7. Stravinsky
8. Schumann
9. Brahms
10. Schubert
11. Handel
12. Debussy

This is a simple numbered list.
1. Beethoven
2. Tchaikovsky
3. Bach
4. Chopin
5. Mozart
6. Schoenberg
7. Haydn
8. Stravinsky
9. Schumann
10. Brahms
11. Schubert
12. Handel
13. Debussy

Automatic Numbered Lists

Unless you have changed a setting in your Pages preferences, you can also start a list by simply numbering the first line with 1. and then pressing Return at the end of that line. The line will be converted to the first line of a numbered list, and the second line will be numbered automatically.

Why Use Numbered Lists?

There are two primary advantages to using a numbered list instead of simply entering a set of lines that start with a number. The first is that you can continue to add items to the list and the numbers will be added automatically. The second is that you can add, insert, or delete items from the list and the numbers will adjust themselves automatically.

Creating Nested Lists

So far we have only looked at lists that are one level deep. But what if you want to have subitems for each item? That's a pretty common need, and here is how to do it.

1. Create a bullet list.

2. Position the text cursor at the end of an item where you want to add subitems.

3. Press Return to start a new line. Then press Tab to make that new line a subitem of the previous item. Now type the item.

4. Continue to type more lines; they remain at the sublevel of the previous item.

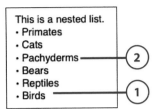

Nested List Levels

You can use the Tab key to increase or decrease the level of indentation. To move a line deeper in the nested list, press Tab. To move it up a level, press Shift-Tab. Other items may be affected by a change. For instance, in this example if you press the Tab key while the text cursor is in the Pachyderms line, then that becomes a subitem of Cats, and the four subitems each get one level deeper, so they remain subitems of Pachyderms.

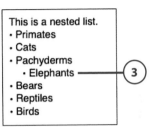

5. Bring up the Inspector window and go to the Text inspector, List category. There you can see the exact level of the line selected, and you can change it here as well.

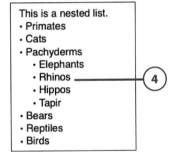

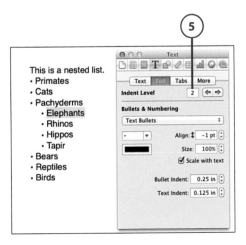

Creating Outlines

You can also make nested numbered lists. These are also commonly known as outlines. Each level can have its own style of numbering. For instance, Roman numerals can be used at the first level, and letters at the second level.

1. Start your outline by typing a list of the main subjects.

2. Click the List Style button.

3. Choose Harvard.

4. The items in the list each have a roman numeral in front of them.

5. Press Return after the first item. Then press the Tab key to indent the new line underneath that first item as a subitem.

6. Enter in three more lines of items.

7. Notice that these lines are all subitems of the first line, and they use capital letters instead of roman numerals. This is the default Harvard list style.

8. You can use the Inspector to change the numbering type for a level of your list. Select the items you want to change and then use the Bullets & Numbering pull-down menus to select a new numbering system.

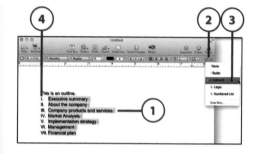

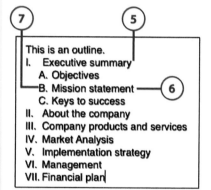

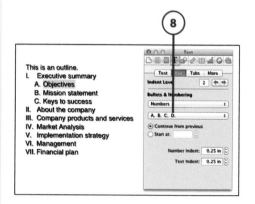

Outlines Versus Outline Mode

In the section "Using Outline Mode" in Chapter 5, " Document Formatting and Organization," we looked at a different type of outline. Outline mode is a writing tool that helps you organize your paragraphs. You can switch between outline mode and regular mode while you organize. But outline lists like in this example are used when you want to have the outline as a part of your document, for the reader to view as an outline.

Customizing Lists

Continuing with the previous example, let's use the Inspector to further customize our outline.

1. Select the entire list.

2. In the Inspector, under Text Inspector, List, choose Tiered Numbers.

3. Now you can choose from one of many styles of tiered numbers. Choose capital letters.

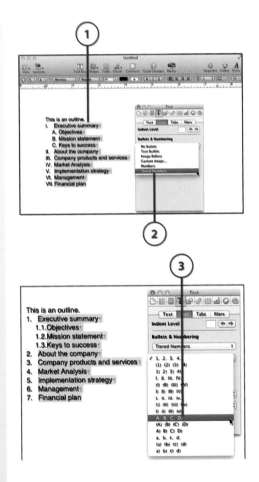

4. Not only are the top-level items changed to use capital letters, but the second-level items are as well. Because A.A. looks kind of ugly, lets change that.

5. Select the three lines of the second level under item A.

6. Use the Inspector to change the style of those items from Tiered Numbers to just Numbers.

7. The second level of items under A now uses numbers.

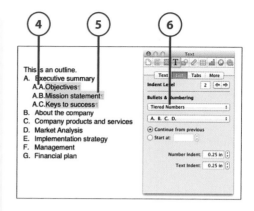

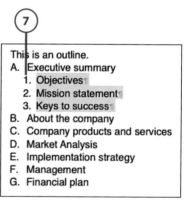

It's Not All Good

Custom Outline Headaches

Unfortunately, a change you make to one subsection of an outline isn't applied to others. Therefore, if you change the subitems under A to use numbers, the subitems under B will not change. You'll have to change those separately. You'll find that it is best to use one of the default list styles, such as Harvard, at first and then adjust the numbering styles when you are done.

Using Custom Bullets

You can also customize the bullets in bullet lists. You can use one of many symbols, any character, or even an image.

1. Start with a simple list.

2. Select the items in the list.

3. Bring up the Inspector and go to Text Inspector, List.

4. Choose a different symbol for the bullet.

5. You can also enter a character directly into this field to use almost anything you want as a bullet.

6. You can set the bullet color by clicking here to bring up the color chooser.

7. If the character you choose doesn't line up nicely with the text, you can adjust its vertical position.

8. You can also increase or decrease the size of the bullet.

9. This setting determines if the bullet size changes along with the font size you use in the list.

10. This setting determines the horizontal location of the bullet.

11. If the bullet is too large and doesn't leave enough space between it and the text, you can move the text of each item over a bit.

12. You can use colorful images as bullets by changing the bullet style.

13. Choose from a variety of full color bullets such as orbs and check boxes.

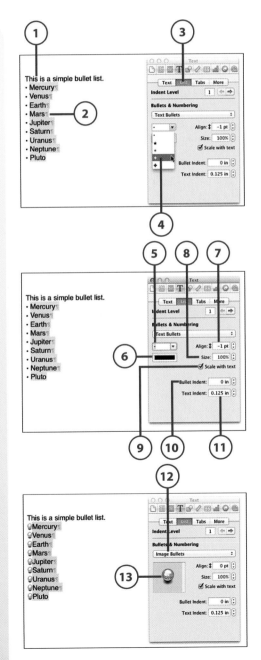

Mix It Up!

You don't have to choose the same bullets for each item in the list. If you want to highlight a particular item, you could choose a different bullet or simply a different bullet color.

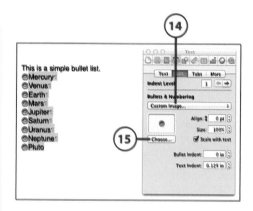

14. You can also choose to use a Custom Image for a bullet.

15. Click here to bring up the Open dialog and choose any image file.

Breaking Up a Numbered List

One of the most difficult things to do with lists is to break them up with extra text. For instance, suppose you want to have items 1 to 4 of a list, then some text, and then items 5 through 9. You need to make sure the two parts of the list, though separated, will number the items properly.

1. Start with a simple numbered list.

2. Position the text cursor at the end of a line and press Return to start a new line.

3. You now have a new item in the list. To delete that item and instead create a break in the list, press Delete.

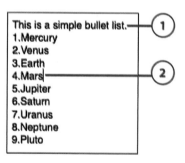

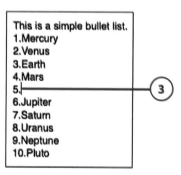

4. Now that you have a break in your list, you can add some text. Notice that the numbering picks up right where it left off.

5. In the Inspector, with the text cursor placed in item number 5, you can see that by default the Continue from Previous option is selected. This is what makes the list numbering continue.

6. At the end of the list, press Return and then Delete to end the list. Then add some more text and continue the list.

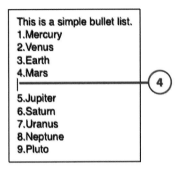

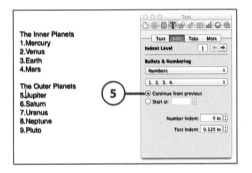

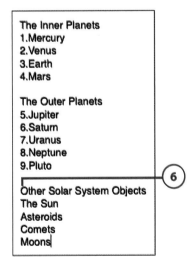

7. Select the new list items.

8. Select the Numbers list type.

9. Notice that the numbering starts fresh and doesn't continue from the previous list. Unfortunately, this is the way that Pages works. It doesn't associate the third part of the list with the first two because the third part was started separately.

10. Delete that third part of your list and instead insert the four new items at the end of the second part of the list.

11. Press Return to go to a new line and then press Delete to create a break in the list. Add more text between the parts of the list.

12. The list now continues normally.

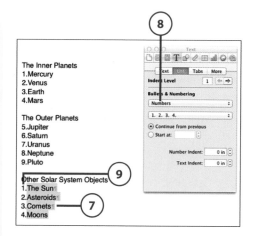

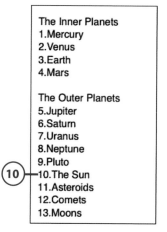

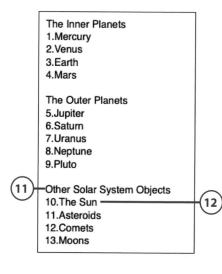

Start At

Sometimes it is difficult to continue a list with a break in between items. You can use the Start At option instead of the Continue from Previous option and manually enter starting numbers for each list section. This isn't always ideal, because inserting an item in one of the early sections of the list means you will have to adjust later sections manually. However, sometimes this is your best choice.

Creating text boxes

Wrapping text around boxes

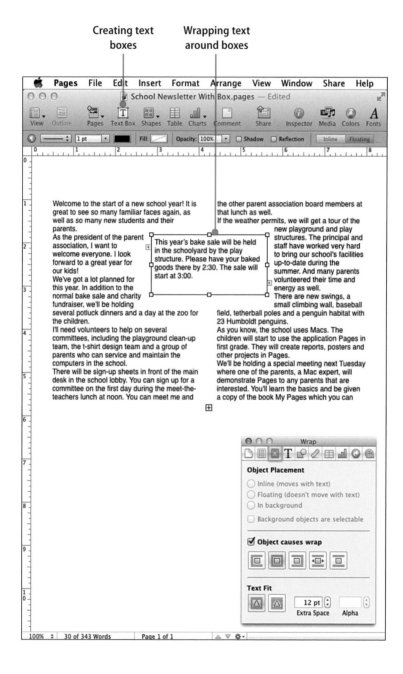

In this chapter, learn how to create and place text boxes in page layout documents, including:

→ Creating and moving text boxes
→ Adding borders to text boxes
→ Wrapping text around text boxes
→ Linking text boxes
→ Using alignment guides
→ Alignment and distribution

Using Text Boxes

The primary element of most page layout documents is the text box. Text boxes are areas that you can fill with text. They can be large, covering the whole page, or small for a title or photo caption. You can mix different text boxes on a page to create posters, newsletters, flyers, or other creative documents. You can also link text boxes together, letting the text flow from one box to another.

Creating and Moving Text Boxes

Let's start by creating a simple text box and placing it in a page layout document.

1. Create a new page layout document and select the Blank Canvas template.

2. Click the Text Box button on the toolbar.

3. A text box is created in the center of your page.

4. Type some text in the box. You may need to click on it once to select it, and then again to put the text cursor in it.

5. Click outside of the text box to deselect it.

6. Click the text box to select it again, only clicking once, which should select the text box for moving and resizing.

7. Click and drag from inside the text box to reposition it.

8. Click and drag any of the corner or side boxes to resize the text box.

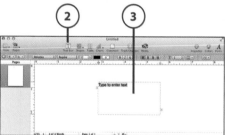

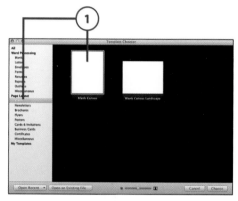

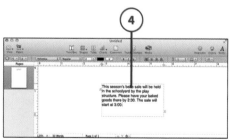

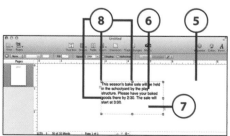

Text Inside Text Boxes

The text inside any text box is just like text in a word processing document. You can style it, size it, and color it. You can use text alignment and tabs. You can even add columns or make bullet lists.

Adding Borders to Text Boxes

Once you have a text box, you can apply styles to the box itself with borders and background colors.

1. Select the text box.

2. Bring up the Inspector window.

3. Select the Graphic inspector.

4. Choose a Line stroke to create a border around the text box.

5. Now you can choose a line type. For instance, you can choose a dashed line or a dotted line instead of a solid one.

6. Choose a color for the border.

7. You can choose a line size for the border.

Shadow Boxing

If you want a text box to pop out of the page, you can also set a shadow for the box. You have a lot of control over the look of the shadow: angle, offset, blur, and opacity. Play around with these controls to create the desired effect.

8. One problem with adding a border is that the text is too close to it. To create a margin around the inside of the box, switch to the Text inspector.

9. Select Text.

10. Increase the Inset Margin slider.

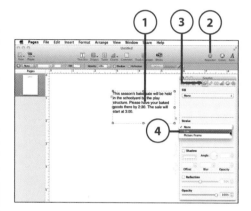

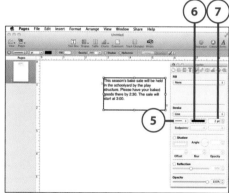

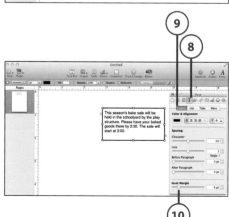

11. To give the box a background color, return to the Graphic inspector.

12. Choose Color Fill as the Fill type.

13. Click to bring up the color chooser and select a color.

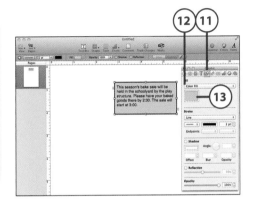

Box Reflections

If you turn on Reflection, you get an effect similar to what Apple uses in iTunes and on its website. The box seems to be reflected from below, like it is standing at the edge of a still lake.

Wrapping Text Around Text Boxes

You can place text boxes on top of other text boxes. As freely movable objects, they can be arranged however you want. Often, you'll need to flow text around a second text box.

1. In a blank page layout document, create a large text box and fill it with text.

2. Set the text box to use two columns.

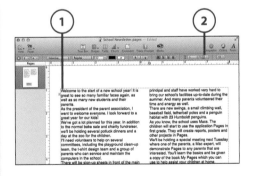

3. Create a second text box similar to the one used in the previous task. Place it right in the middle of the other text box. Make sure it is selected.

4. Bring up the Inspector window.

5. Go to the Wrap inspector.

6. Check the Object Causes Wrap option.

7. You should use the default wrap style, which causes the text to flow around the box on all sides.

8. You can set the amount of space around the text box to your liking.

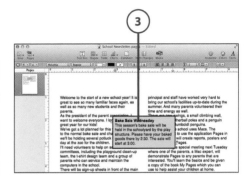

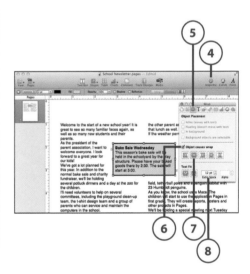

Front to Back

When you have multiple items in a layout, each item appears either in front of or behind other items. If the large text box in this example were in front of the small one, you would not be able to select the small one. In that case, you select the large one and choose Arrange, Send Backward or Arrange Send to Back to send the large text box to the back. Then, you can select the small text box, which will now be in front.

Linking Text Boxes

The key to designing a page layout document is to be able to place text boxes in different parts of the page and then link them together. This lets text flow from one box to the other, as it might in a newspaper or magazine.

1. Create a new page layout document.

2. Add a text box.

3. Add some text to the text box, preferably more text than can fit in the text box in its current size.

4. Move the text box over to the left.

5. Enlarge the text box a bit vertically by dragging down the square in the middle of the bottom side.

6. Create a new text box and place it under the first, stretching it to span across the entire page. This might be how you would arrange things if you planned to put some other element such as a photo in the upper-right corner.

7. Click the link handle at the lower-right corner of the first text box.

8. Click anywhere in the second text box to link it. The text now flows from the first text box to the second. Inserting new text into the first will automatically update both text boxes and reflow the text as you type.

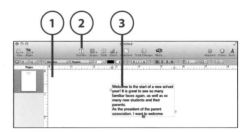

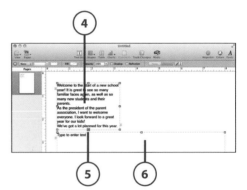

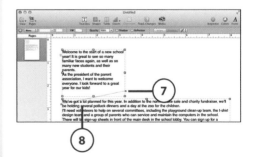

9. Bring up the Inspector window.

10. Select the Text inspector.

11. Click More.

12. Notice that the text flows such that a paragraph is not divided between the text box. You can change how text flows from one box to the other with these options.

13. If you want to link the second text box to a third one, click the link handle and repeat steps 7 and 8.

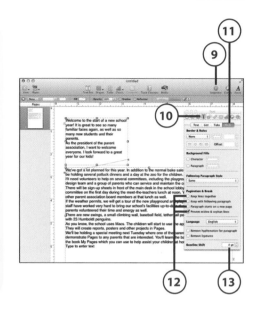

From Page to Page

You would most commonly use text box links to flow the text from one page to another. For instance, an article in a magazine document could flow from page 4 to 5, and then the article can jump from page 5 to page 23 at the back of the magazine.

Using Alignment Guides

In a page layout document, you can move your text boxes, shapes, and images around as you please. But creating nice documents usually requires precision. You want to make sure your boxes and other elements line up with each other properly.

Fortunately, there is an easy way to do this in Pages. Alignment guides appear as you drag elements and let you lock element positions to each other.

1. Choose Pages, Preferences. Then choose Rulers preferences.

2. Make sure both kinds of guides are turned on.

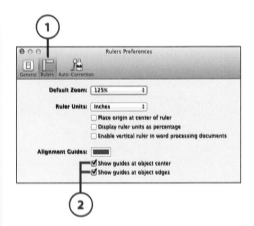

View the Layout

To use guides, you must make the layout of the page visible. Choose View, Show Layout. This also allows you to see the edges of the page.

3. Create a text box and then drag it around on the page.

4. You'll notice a blue line appear when your box is near the center of the page. The box will lock to that guide if you are dragging it close to the line. This allows you to place a text box at precisely the center of the page.

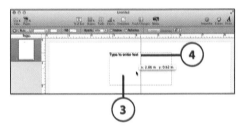

5. Create a second text box and drag that around.

6. If you try to align the second box under the first, guides appear and lock the second text box to the first, as long as you are close to aligning them as you drag.

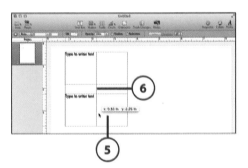

7. Click in the ruler at the left or top side of the page. If you do not see any rulers, choose View, Show Rulers.

8. As you drag, a guide is created, and you can place it where you want on the page.

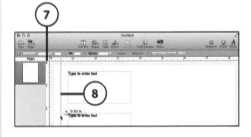

9. Drag a text box so that the left side approximately touches one of the guides.

10. The text box snaps to the guide you have created, making it easy to align that box and others to a specific position on the page.

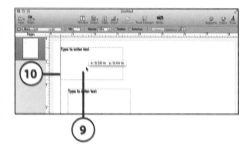

Temporary Guides

Alignment guides can help you align boxes and other elements in all sorts of ways. You can align sides and centers of elements to each other or to the guides you create. You can drag the existing guides later on to get them out of the way or to reposition them.

Alignment and Distribution

In addition to using guides, you can align and distribute objects using some simple commands.

1. Create three text boxes in a page layout document. Select them.

2. Choose Arrange, Align Objects, Middle.

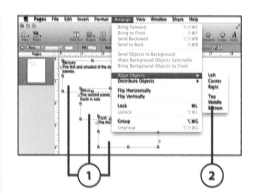

3. The three text boxes are now aligned vertically.

4. Choose Arrange, Distribute Objects, Horizontally.

5. The three boxes are now equally distributed horizontally, using the entire document space.

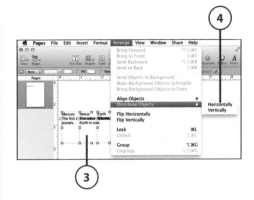

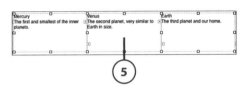

>>>Go Further

ALIGNMENT PRACTICE

To get a better understanding of the automatic alignment features in Pages, create a blank page layout document. Then create several text boxes. Now play around with dragging them horizontally and vertically. See how they lock to eack other's edges and centers. Try changing the size of some of the text boxes and dragging them. After a while you get a good feel of how easily you can drag items around and have them line up with each other.

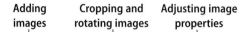

Adding images   Cropping and rotating images   Adjusting image properties

In this chapter, you'll learn all about adding images to your documents, including:

- → Adding images to word processing documents
- → Setting image borders
- → Cropping an image
- → Fitting text around images
- → Rotating an image
- → Adjusting the image color and quality
- → Using an image as a background

Adding Images

After mastering text in Pages, the next natural step is to learn how to add and manipulate images. Simply adding an image to a document is just the beginning. You'll want to know how to resize the image, add borders, wrap text around it, and adjust the image quality.

Adding Images to Word Processing Documents

In the section "Adding Images" in Chapter 2, "Working with Page Layout Documents," you learned the basics of adding an image to a page layout document. Let's start by adding an image to a word processing document. You then learn how to wrap text around the image.

1. Open an existing document.

2. Place the cursor at the location where you want the image to appear.

3. Choose Insert, Choose.

4. Use the Open dialog to locate the image you want to import.

5. Click Insert.

6. The image will appear in the document.

7. Use the squares in the corners and the middle of the sides to resize the image.

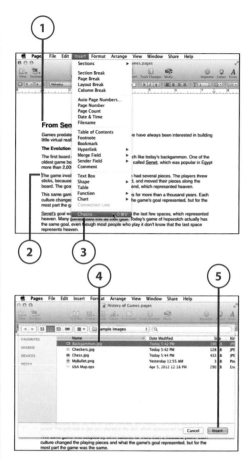

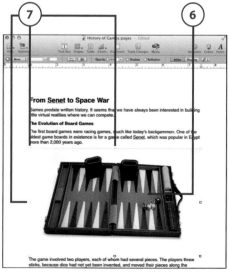

8. The image now appears smaller. Notice how the start of the next paragraph begins at the lower-right corner of the image. This is because the image is actually in the text, and that line is the very next thing after the image.

9. Bring up the Inspector.

10. Choose the Wrap inspector.

11. Here you find the setting to make the image "inline" as part of the text, like any other character. You can change the image so that it floats above the text or floats in the background.

12. Turn on Object Causes Wrap. This causes the text to flow around the image.

13. Set the wrapping so that the text flows to the left of the image.

14. The image is now on the right side of the text, with the text flowing around to the left. Experiment using other text-wrapping settings to see where the image sits and how the text flows around it.

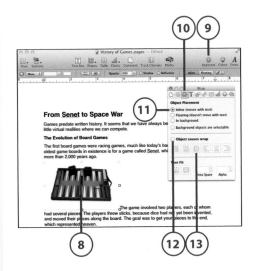

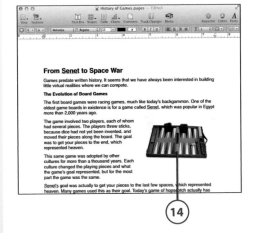

>>>Go Further

WAYS TO IMPORT IMAGES

There are many ways to get an image into your documents. Pick the one that works best for you in any given situation.

Menu bar—Choose Insert, Choose and then select a file.

Drag from Finder—Drag an image file from a Finder window or the desktop into the document window.

Media browser—Click the Media button on the Pages toolbar and then select a picture from your iPhoto library.

Drag from iPhoto—You can also drag a photo from iPhoto directly into the Pages document window.

Copy and paste—You can copy an image file or part of an image from inside a graphics program and then paste it into your Pages document. You can even Control-click and copy an image from a web page and then paste it into your document.

Setting Image Borders

You can use a variety of image borders, including simple lines and picture frames. You can also use shadows and reflections.

Using a Simple Line Border

For most purposes, a simple border works best. If you want to get a little fancier, you can choose a line type that looks more like a magic marker than a perfect line. You can also set the color of the border.

1. Select an image in a word processing document.

2. Bring up the Inspector window.

3. Select the Graphic inspector.

4. Choose the stroke type Line.

5. Choose a line type. In this example, a jagged border is chosen.

6. Choose the border color.

7. Set the border size.

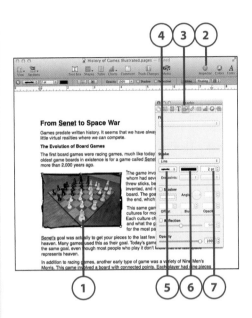

Using a Picture Frame

A more elaborate type of image border is the picture frame. These tend to make the image look like it has been pasted into your document in a scrapbook-like manner.

1. Select the image.

2. Bring up the Inspector window.

3. Choose the Graphic inspector.

4. Select the stroke type Picture Frame.

5. You can choose from one of many types of picture frames.

6. To further customize the look of the frame, try adjusting its scale. In this case, a scale of 50% looks much better than the default 100%.

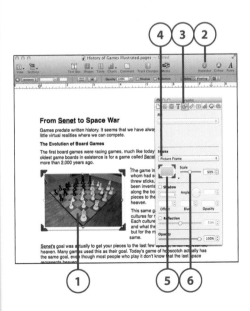

Using Picture Shadows

Another way to make your images more interesting is to have them cast a shadow on the page. In this example, we just use a shadow. However, you can also combine shadows with line or picture frames.

1. Select the image.

2. Bring up the Inspector window.

3. Choose the Graphic inspector.

4. Turn on the Shadow effect.

5. Set a color for the shadow. Usually black is best, but if your document is dominated by another color, you might want to try that color as an alternative.

6. The angle determines from which direction the light source is coming. For example, an angle of 315 degrees casts the shadow to the lower right. An angle of 135 degrees casts the shadow to the upper left.

7. The offset is how far from the center the shadow lies, according to the angle. For example, an offset of 0 makes it appear as if the light is coming directly down on the page, thus causing a slight shadow to appear on all sides. An offset of 6 puts the shadow almost completely off to the side specified by the angle.

8. Blur specifies how fuzzy the shadow will look. A setting of 1 creates a very crisp, defined shadow. A setting of 10 or higher creates a blurry, more natural shadow.

9. You can also lighten or darken the shadow by setting the opacity amount.

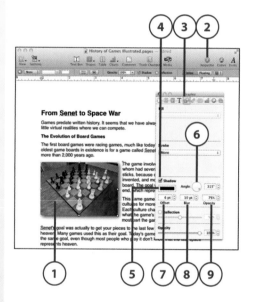

Using Picture Reflections

Another effect you can use with pictures is the reflection. This effect reflects the bottom of the picture in a virtual mirror just below the picture itself. It is kind of like having the picture standing at the side of a still body of water.

You can combine the refection with any or all of the following effects: borders, frames, and shadows.

1. Select the image.

2. Bring up the Inspector window.

3. Choose the Graphic inspector.

4. Turn on the Reflection option.

5. Set the reflection amount. The default of 50% creates a partially faded reflection. Choosing a higher number will make the reflection stronger.

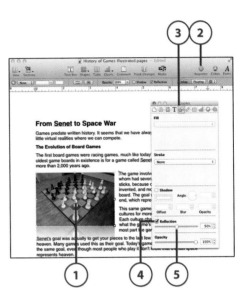

Cropping an Image

If you don't want to use all of an image, you can crop the image so that you only use a portion of it.

1. Select an image in a document.

2. Choose Format, Mask.

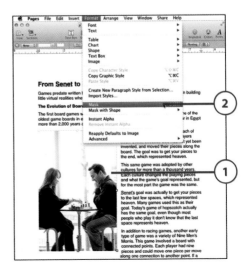

3. Click and drag the image to position it. Only the portion of the image in the box will be visible when you are done masking the image.

4. Shrink or enlarge the image to fit more or less of it in the box.

5. Drag the corners and edges of the box to change its dimensions.

6. Use the Edit Mask button to switch back and forth between this mode and the regular mode where you can move and scale the image.

7. Alternatively, click outside of the image to deselect it and see the results of your changes.

8. Only a portion of the image is shown now that it has been cropped.

9. Once you have masked an image, you can select it and you'll get the scale and Edit Mask button below so that you can make adjustments.

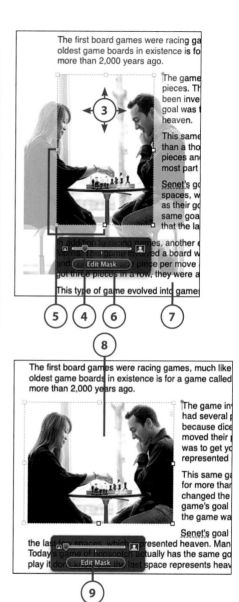

Masking an Image with a Shape

You can also choose Format, Mask with Shape and then choose a shape such as an oval or rounded rectangle. This crops the image and places it inside the shape. The masking controls from that point on are similar to a normal mask, although you may also get controls to adjust the shape, such as a dot you can grab to adjust the roundness of the corners of a rounded rectangle.

Fitting Text Around Images

You have already seen how to wrap text around a rectangular image. But what if the image has plenty of white space and you want to wrap the text tightly to the shape of the image?

You can do that in Pages using either an image with a semitransparent background or an image that has clearly defined white space.

1. Select an image in a document. For the purposes of this example, we use an image with a lot of obvious white space around a clearly defined object.

2. Bring up the Inspector window.

3. Choose the Wrap inspector.

4. In this case, the image is an inline object, but the same basic steps can be performed with a floating object.

5. The image is set to cause text to wrap around it.

6. The wrap will flow text around the right side of the image.

7. Set the Text Fit option so that the wrap follows the contour of the object.

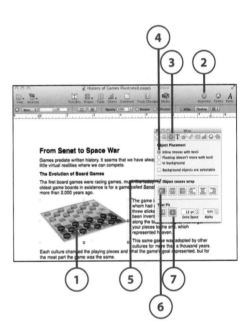

USING SEMITRANSPARENT IMAGES

Go Further

If you are lucky enough to be using a semitransparent image, fitting text closely around it becomes easy. A semitransparent image is a 32-bit graphic that has an *alpha channel* (a measurement of transparency for each pixel). Thus, Pages knows which parts of the image are supposed to be transparent.

Unfortunately, most clipart is not 32 bit with an alpha channel. You will usually find images like this one that simply have a solid color as a background and no indication of transparency. If this were a 32-bit image, the text would fit around the object as soon as you completed step 7.

8. Choose Format, Instant Alpha. This allows you to tell Pages that part of this image is meant to be transparent.

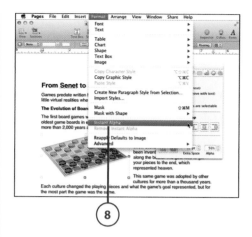

8

9. Now you can click and drag in the image. Do this in an area that is meant to be transparent, such as the white space in this example. As you drag, a circle forms. Any color in this circle becomes transparent throughout the image. While you are dragging, the transparent space is represented by a green color to give you an exact representation of what will be transparent.

9

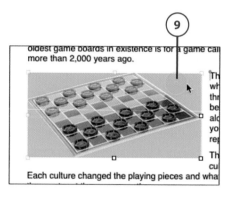

10. When you have finished, the text should wrap around the object, taking the transparency you have defined into account.

10

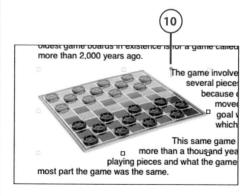

>>>Go Further

DEFINING EXACT SHAPES

With this example, we were lucky that the background was a nice solid white. However, more complex images may make it harder to specify exactly how to wrap the text—but there is a way. In Chapter 9, "Adding Shapes," you learn how to use shapes. You will see how you can put an image into a shape. You also learn how to draw your own custom shapes. You can combine these two techniques to draw a custom shape and then place an image in it. This allows you to crop an image and wrap text around it any way you want, regardless of what the image looks like.

Rotating an Image

Sometimes you need to rotate an image to get the result you want in your document. You can rotate with the Metrics inspector.

1. Select the image.

2. Bring up the Inspector window.

3. Choose the Metrics inspector.

4. You can use the rotation controls or enter in a specific angle to rotate the image.

5. You can also hold down the ⌘ key and drag any corner or side of the image to rotate it in place in the document. In fact, you can do this without even bringing up the Inspector window.

6. You can also flip an image horizontally or vertically.

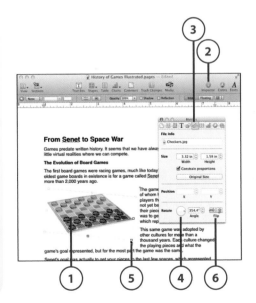

Get It Straight

If you want to quickly rotate an image by 45, 90, or 180 degrees, or some other multiple of 45, you can grab a corner and ⌘-drag while also holding down the Shift key. This locks the angle change to 45-degree intervals.

Adjusting the Image Color and Quality

In a perfect world, all images would look exactly like you want them to look in your Pages documents. Sometimes, though, you have to make adjustments. The same tools that are available in programs such as iPhoto are also available from inside Pages.

1. Select an image in a Pages document.

2. Choose View, Show Adjust Image to bring up the Adjust Image window.

3. Adjust the brightness and contrast of the image.

4. You can adjust the color of the image by changing the saturation, temperature, and tint.

5. Adjust the sharpness.

6. Adjust the exposure.

7. Use the sliders to adjust the color levels in the image.

8. Not sure what to do? If you are not a photographer or graphics professional, a lot of these controls won't mean anything to you. You can instead simply click the Enhance button, which will automatically adjust the image to try to improve its appearance.

9. After playing with the controls for a while, you can use the Reset Image button to return them all to their default settings and start again.

10. The changes to the image happen in real time. So you can watch the image change as you make adjustments. When the image looks the way you want it, simply close the Adjust Image window.

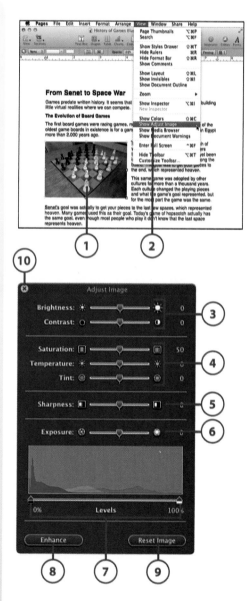

Using an Image as a Background

Occasionally you might want to use an image behind text as a background. You can do this by placing the image behind other objects in a page layout document and setting the image to not cause any text wrapping. For word processing documents, the process is a little different.

1. Bring an image into a word processing document. Don't worry about setting the wrapping properties of the image.

2. Bring up the Inspector window.

3. Choose the Wrap inspector.

4. Change the Object Placement type to In Background.

5. Turn on the Background Objects Are Selectable option to make it easier to select the image for the next steps.

6. Use the corners of the image to stretch it to cover the entire page. It is okay if some of the image stretches beyond the visible portion of the page. Unless the image is the exact same rectangular ratio as the page, that is inevitable.

7. The text is now hard to read because it is black text on a dark background. You could make the text another color, or you could adjust the image. Bring up the Adjust Image window by choosing View, Show Adjust Image.

8. By increasing the brightness and decreasing the contrast, you can create a lighter background. You may also want to experiment with the saturation and exposure settings. The best settings depend on the content of the image.

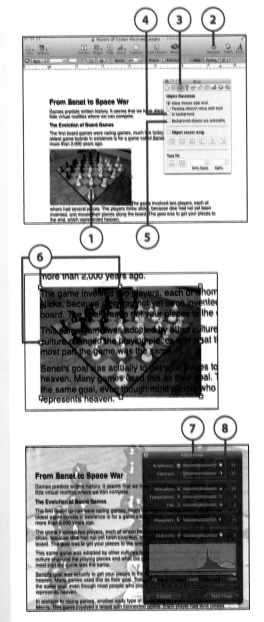

9. Because this background image will tend to get in the way as you try to select text in your document, choose Arrange, Make Background Objects Selectable to turn this option off.

10. Alternatively, you can also lock the image in place, making it impossible to move again until you select it and unlock it.

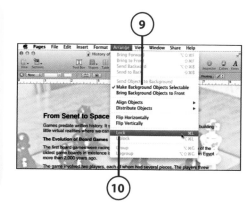

Background for Every Page

If you want to make the background image appear on every page of your document, you need to move it to the Section Master. This is the master page template that every page is based on. You learn more about templates in Chapter 15, "Using and Building Templates."

For now, select the image and choose Format, Advanced, Move Object to Section Master. You'll now see that image on every page of your document.

Placing text and
images in a shape

Adding
shapes

Adjusting shape
borders

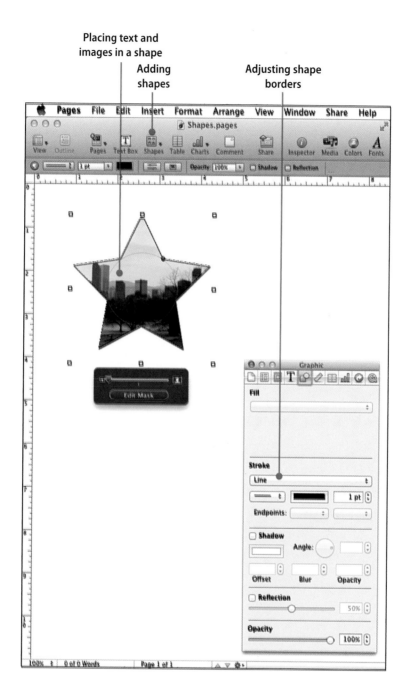

In this chapter, you'll learn about using shapes and how they can enhance your documents, including:

→ Creating a shape
→ Adding text to shapes
→ Adding images to shapes
→ Using shapes in documents
→ Custom shapes
→ Copying shape styles

Adding Shapes

You can add rectangles, circles, stars, arrows, and other elements to your documents. Each shape can have its own color, border, and other visual properties. You can adjust the size of shapes and leave them empty, or put text or pictures in.

Creating a Shape

A basic shape can easily be added to either a word processing or page layout document. Let's work with a page layout document to create a shape and set its basic visual properties.

1. Start with a blank page layout
   document.

2. Click the Shapes button on the
   toolbar.

3. Choose a shape.

4. The shape will appear in your
   document. You can click and drag
   it to any position on the page.

5. You can click and drag any of the
   corners or the sides to resize the
   shape.

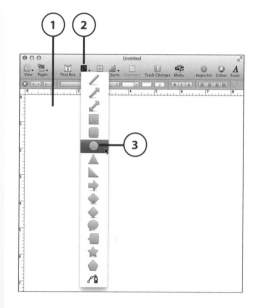

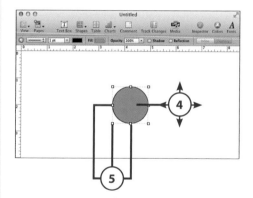

6. Bring up the Inspector window.

7. Go to the Graphic inspector.

8. Set the type of fill for the shape. You can choose None for no fill, or even select a gradient or image fill. For this example, leave it as a basic Color Fill.

9. Set the color of the fill by clicking the color chip to bring up the Colors palette.

10. Leave the stroke setting at Line. You can also choose a picture frame, which works best with rectangular shapes, or None for no frame.

11. Set the line style, color, and size.

12. You can add a drop shadow to the shape, just like you can with images.

13. You can also add a reflection.

14. If you would rather make the shape semitransparent, showing some of what is behind it, you can reduce the opacity to something less than 100%.

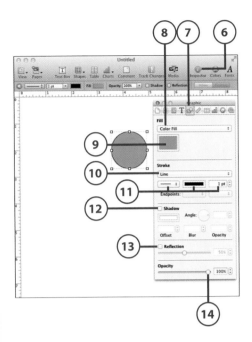

Moving Shapes with the Arrow Keys

With a shape selected, you can move it 1 pixel at a time by pressing the arrow keys on your keyboard. You can use Shift-arrow key to move the shape in larger increments. One Shift-arrow equals 10 arrow key presses.

Using the Format Bar

Most of what you need to work with shapes will appear in the format bar, under the toolbar when a shape is selected, so you don't always need to bring up the Inspector window.

Adding Text to Shapes

A shape is just a text box with a background color and border. You can place text in a shape just like you can in a text box. Text in a shape flows to fit the edges of the shape, so each line wraps when it gets close to the border of the shape.

1. Create a shape and adjust its size as you like in the document.

2. Double-click inside the shape to place the text cursor there.

3. Type or paste text into the shape.

4. Use the toolbar to adjust the text style, size, alignment, and other properties just like you would with any text.

5. Use the corner and side handles to resize the shape. The text will reflow as you resize it.

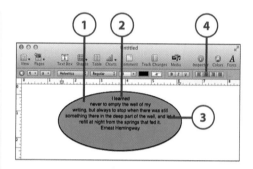

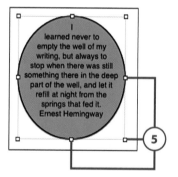

Additional Shape Controls

Some shapes have additional controls that appear when you select them. For instance, the star has a control for the number of points that will appear under it when selected. You can also grab a blue dot in the star that lets you adjust the depth of the points.

Adding Images to Shapes

Shapes can also be used as containers for images. Instead of having the image be a separate element by itself, it can be inserted into a shape, thus creating an unusual frame for the image.

1. Create a shape and place it in the document.

2. Bring up the Media Browser and select Photos.

3. Select an image and drag it from the Media Browser into the document. You could also drag an image from a Finder window or the desktop.

4. Drag the image over the shape. You'll see the shape border change to blue to show that it is the selected destination of the image. Drop the image on the shape.

5. The image is now in the same location as the shape, but masked by the shape. You can edit the mask the same way you did in the section "Cropping an Image" in Chapter 8, "Adding Images."

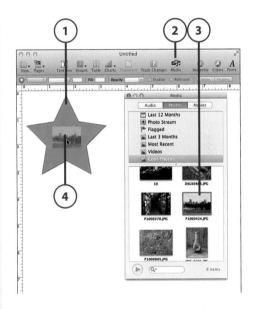

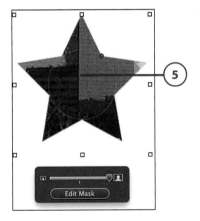

6. Bring up the Inspector window.

7. Go to the Graphic inspector.

8. You can change the stroke, shadow, and other visual properties of the shape, but you can no longer change the fill because the shape is now filled by the image.

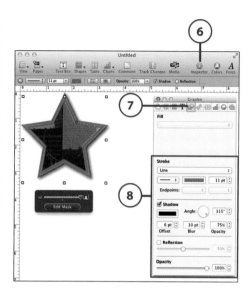

What's the Difference?

There's really no difference between a shape that has been filled with an image and an image that has been masked by a shape. You can get the same results with either approach.

Using Shapes in Documents

You don't always want to have text wrap around shapes. Sometimes you want shapes that coexist with text in the same space. In this example, we add a line and an arrow that fits in with the text.

1. Start with a word processing document.

2. Add a shape from the toolbar.

3. Select a plain line shape.

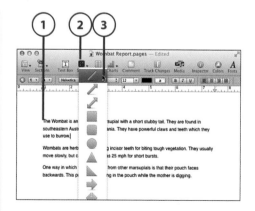

4. The line will appear in the center of the page.

5. Use the format bar to change its type to a thick fuzzy line.

6. Bring up the Inspector window.

7. Go to the Wrap inspector.

8. Turn off object wrapping.

9. Move the line to under a word that you want to emphasize. Shrink it to fit just under the word.

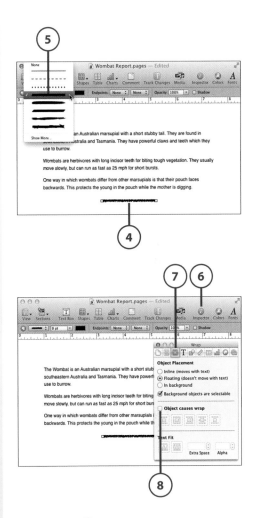

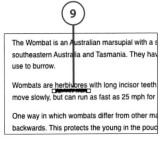

10. Create another shape, this time an arrow.

11. Set its style.

12. Turn off its object wrapping.

13. Position the arrow shape so one end comes from the center of the line, and the other points to a space to the right side of the page.

14. Create a third shape, this time a rectangle. Make the line the same type as the arrow, but set the fill color to white. This time we do not turn off wrapping because we want the text to wrap around it. Add some text.

In reality, you'll want to make the arrow a little less obtrusive, perhaps by changing its color to a gray or making it 50% opaque. You could also set the object placement in the inspector to In Background to have black text appear on top of the gray or semi-transparent arrow.

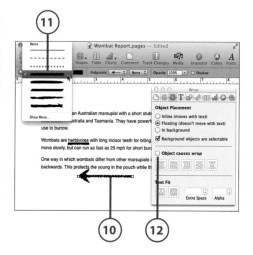

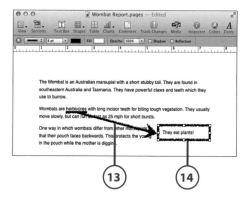

Rotating Shapes

For shapes such as triangles and arrows, you can get more variety by simply rotating them. You do this in the same way as you have learned to do for images. Just ⌘-drag the corners or use the Metrics inspector.

Custom Shapes

In addition to rectangles, circles, stars, bubbles, arrows, and other basic shapes, Pages also allows you to create your own shapes by drawing with a series of points.

Creating a Basic Custom Shape

The most basic kind of custom shape simply uses a series of points to define a set of lines.

1. Open a new page layout document.

2. Add a new shape.

3. Select a custom shape.

4. Click anywhere on the page to start drawing. Use just a quick single click.

5. Click again to place a second point. This will connect the first point with the second with a line. Continue to click to add new lines to the shape.

6. To end your drawing and create a solid shape, click one last time at the same point where you started.

7. With the finished shape selected, you can set shape properties such as line size, fill color, and shadows.

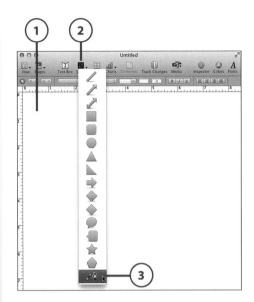

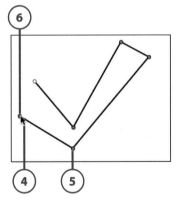

Closed or Open?

You don't need to complete the shape by finishing on the same point where you started. Instead, you can just press the Esc key on the keyboard and leave the shape unclosed. You won't be able to fill the shape with a color because it has no "inside." However, you can still set the line properties.

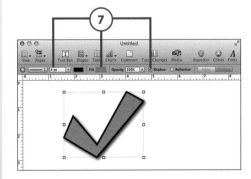

Creating a Custom Shape with Curves

You can also create slightly more complex shapes using curves. A curve has two points, just like a line. However, one or both of those points also has vector handles to produce a curved path.

1. Start drawing a shape as before. Place the first point.

2. Click to place the second point, but continue to hold the mouse button or trackpad down.

3. Drag away from the point, and the two vector handles will appear.

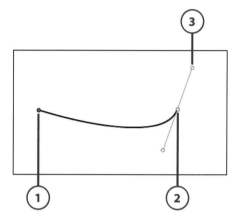

From here, you can continue to add more points. You can make any point a curved vector point or a noncurved point. Using this technique to draw curves can be frustrating if you have never used a vector drawing program before. Usually only professional graphic artists use them.

Modifying a Regular Shape

You can also take a regular shape, such as a circle or rectangle, and turn it into a custom shape and then edit it.

1. Create a normal shape, such as this arrow.

2. Choose Format, Shape, Make Editable.

3. Now you'll have points, just as if the shape were created as a custom shape.

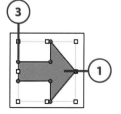

4. You can click to select a red dot. Shift-click carefully to select a second one. Then drag those dots to modify the shape. You can select one or many dots in any shape and drag them together.

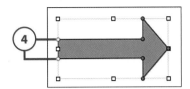

Copying Shape Styles

Suppose you create a shape and then style it using a line type, color, fill, shadow, and so on. You get the look you like and decide you want to use the same style for other shapes in your document. You don't have to re-create the style step by step. Instead, you can copy and paste the style from one shape to the next.

1. Create a shape.

2. Set it up with the style you want.

3. Create a second shape.

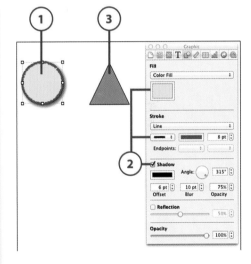

4. With the first shape selected, choose Format, Copy Graphic Style.

5. With the second shape selected, choose Format, Paste Graphic Style.

6. The second shape takes on all the style properties of the first shape.

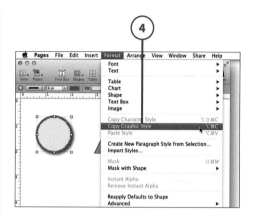

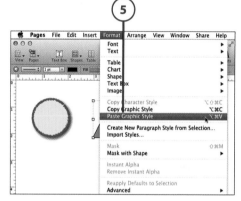

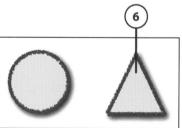

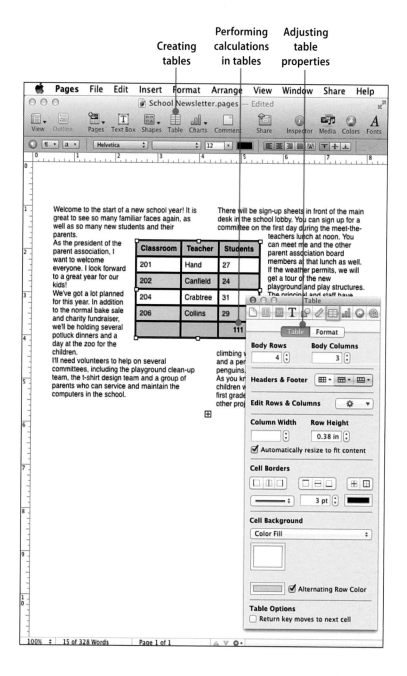

Creating
tables

Performing
calculations
in tables

Adjusting
table
properties

In this chapter, you'll learn how to use tables in your documents, including:

→ Adding a basic table
→ Customizing tables
→ Performing calculations in tables
→ Using table headers and footers
→ Table cell formatting

10

Creating Tables

Another type of element you can add to either word processing or page layout documents is a table of numbers or information. You can also add a chart—either a line or bar graph or a pie chart. These can fit into your document like an image or a shape, or they can comprise the entire document.

Adding a Basic Table

Tables are little spreadsheets, similar to what you would create in Numbers or Microsoft Excel. You can use them in either word processing or page layout documents.

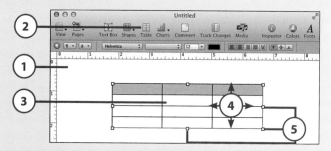

1. Create a blank page layout document.

2. Click the Table button on the toolbar.

3. A basic 3-by-4 table will appear in the middle of your document.

4. You can click and drag the table to another location on the page.

5. You can drag the corners or edges to resize the table. This doesn't add or remove cells in the table; instead, it just stretches the entire table.

6. Double-click in a cell to move the text cursor there. Enter in the text for that cell.

7. To move to another cell, you can double-click in it or use the Tab key to jump to it.

8. The gray cells at the top are header cells. Text in them will appear bold. This cell is a body cell, which has a white background and plain text.

9. To add another row, choose Format, Table, Add Row Below. You can also add a row above or add columns.

MOVING AROUND IN TABLES

To move from cell to cell in a table, you can simply rely on double-clicking to place the text cursor in the cell. A single click will select the cell, and then typing will replace the contents of the cell with whatever you type.

You can move to the next cell with Tab or to the previous cell with Shift-Tab. Using Tab in the last cell in the lower-right corner automatically starts a new row.

You can also navigate with the arrow keys. If the text cursor is inside text in a cell, an arrow key will simply move the text cursor. However, if the text cursor is before the first character of text in a cell, or after the last character, one more arrow press will move to the previous or next cell. You can use up- and down-arrow keys to move up and down the rows.

TABLES ARE LIKE IMAGES AND SHAPES

You can place tables just like you can place images and shapes. You can put them in word processing documents or page layout documents. Also, you can set text to wrap around them with the same Wrap inspector options.

Welcome to the start of a new school year! It is great to see so many familiar faces again, as well as so many new students and their parents. As the president of the parent association, I want to welcome everyone. I look forward to a great year for our kids! We've got a lot planned for this year. In addition to the normal bake sale and charity fundraiser, we'll be holding several potluck dinners and a day at the zoo for the children. I'll need volunteers to help on several committees, including the playground clean-up team, the t-shirt design team and a group of parents who can service and maintain the computers in the school.

Classroom	Teacher	Students
201	Hand	27
202	Canfield	24
204	Crabtree	31
206	Collins	29
		111

There will be sign-up sheets in front of the main desk in the school lobby. You can sign up for a committee on the first day during the meet-the-teachers lunch at noon. You can meet me and the other parent association board members at that lunch as well. If the weather permits, we will get a tour of the new playground and play structures. The principal and staff have worked very hard to bring our school's facilities up-to-date during the summer. And many parents volunteered their time and energy as well. There are new swings, a small climbing wall, baseball field, tetherball poles and a penguin habitat at 23 Humboldt penguins. As you know, the school uses Macs. The children will start to use the application Pages in first grade. They will create reports, posters and other projects in Pages.

Here you can see text in two columns and a table in the center. The table is set to Object Causes Wrap, and wrapping is allowed on all sides.

Customizing Tables

You can highly customize the look of your table using the Inspector window. Some controls affect the entire table, whereas others affect only the cells, rows, or columns selected.

1. Create a basic table and fill it with some values.

2. Bring up the Inspector window.

3. Go to the Table inspector.

4. Click Table.

5. You can use the Inspector to change the number of rows and columns.

6. A default table has one header row, denoted by its gray background and bold, centered text. However, you can add more header rows, header columns on the left, and footer rows at the bottom. In the upcoming task "Using Table Headers and Footers," you'll see what makes these special.

7. You can change the appearance of the cell borders, adding and removing them from the selected cells as well as setting their style, size, and color.

8. You can also change the background color of the selected cells.

9. This option lets you define a second row color that will be used in every other row.

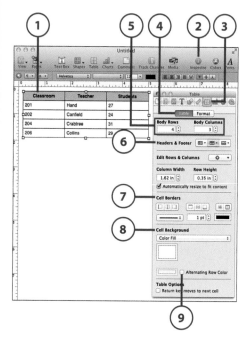

10. Here's an example of a custom-ized table. You can see the chang-es reflected in the Inspector: thicker borders, a footer row, and alternate row colors.

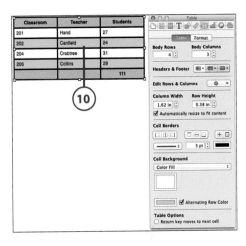

>>>Go Further

WIDTH AND HEIGHT CHANGES

If you need to change the width of a column in your table, you can do it by just dragging the line between the column to the left or right. The lines will even snap to other elements on the page just like moving text boxes or shapes. You can also drag the lines between rows to change the height of a row.

To change the width or height of columns and rows in the table uniformly, you can select multiple cells in the table and then use the Column Width and Column Height controls in the Inspector window.

Performing Calculations in Tables

Because tables are just little spreadsheets, it follows that you can use formu-las to perform calculations.

Simple Math

Let's start by using simple math to multiple two numbers together.

1. Create a simple table and add some data, like in this example.

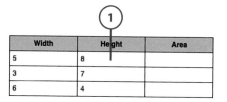

2. Double-click in the C2 cell and start by typing =. This brings up a black oval box with an X and a check mark in it. This lets you know you are entering a formula.

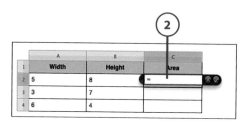

3. One way to enter a formula is just by typing. In this case, you can type **A2*B2**. The * is the computer math symbol for multiplication. Notice how the cells A2 and B2 change colors to match the entries you are typing. This color change is only a temporary visual cue while entering the formula.

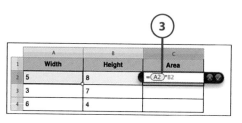

4. Another way to enter a formula is to use a combination of typing and clicking. Start by typing = as you did in step 2.

5. Click cell A2, and the A2 will be inserted into the formula.

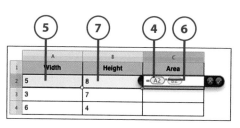

6. Type the * symbol.

7. Click cell B2, and the B2 will be inserted into the formula.

8. Whether you used step 3, or steps 4, 5, 6, and 7, you can complete the formula by pressing Return or clicking the green check mark button. The result of the calculation is then shown in the cell.

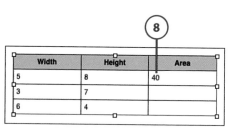

9. You can change a value in one of the cells that the formula depends on, and the result will instantly be updated after you are done changing the cell's value.

10. Select and copy (⌘-C) the cell with the formula in it.

11. Select each cell under it in that row and paste (⌘-V) into it. The formula will be pasted there and will automatically adjust to being in a different row. The results in those cells will match the values of the cells in the columns to the left of each one.

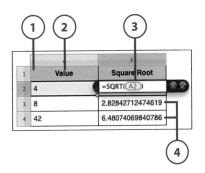

Width	Height	Area
7	8	56
3	7	21
6	4	24

Math Symbols

In addition to using * for multiplication, you use / for division. The + and – symbols are used for addition and subtraction. And you can also use parentheses to group calculations such as (A2+B2)*C3. You can insert regular numbers, as well (for example, A2*7+B2-5).

Using Special Functions

In Pages, you also have access to a variety of mathematical functions. You can use these in tables to perform complex calculations.

1. Create a simple table with two columns.

2. In the first column, enter some sample numbers.

3. In the first cell in the second column, enter the formula =SQRT(A2).

4. Copy and paste the formula in the rest of the cells in the B column.

	Value	Square Root
1		
2	4	=SQRT(A2)
3	8	2.82842712474619
4	42	6.48074069840786

5. For an easily remembered function such as SQRT, you can just type in the function. However, for other functions you can bring up the Functions Browser by choosing Insert, Function, Show Function Browser.

6. Choose from the function categories on the left.

7. Select a function on the right. Alternatively, you can use the search box to jump right to a function.

8. You can read a description of a function and see examples.

9. Click Insert Function to paste the function in the formula you are constructing.

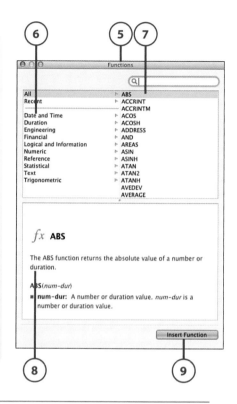

All from Numbers

The formulas you can enter and the functions you can use are all straight from Pages' sibling app, Numbers. In fact, most spreadsheet programs, such as Excel, use the same functions. Therefore, if you are familiar with Excel functions, you should be able to use the functions in Pages and Numbers easily.

Using Table Headers and Footers

The gray cells at the top of most of the examples so far in this chapter have represented the header row. You can also create header columns on the left and footer rows at the bottom. These are much more than simply cells that have a different color and text style.

When you're building a list of data, headers and footers help differentiate between the titles and results of a column. Many functions understand that these parts of your table are different than the cells in the body of the table.

1. Create a simple table with data.

2. Bring up the Inspector window.

3. Go to the Table inspector.

4. Click Table.

5. Click the Footer button.

6. Select 1 to add one footer row.

7. Click in the footer row cell for the C column. Start a formula using the SUM function by typing **=SUM(**. Be sure to include the opening parenthesis.

8. Instead of typing C, click the label C at the top of the third column. This will add the column to the formula, and even use the label Students rather than C in the formula. However, you could type **=SUM** for the same result.

9. Close the function by typing the right parenthesis and then press Return.

10. The sum of the numbers in column C is now displayed in the footer. Because you put the formula in the footer and used a header row for the labels, the formula **=SUM** is smart enough to know not to include the values in the header or footer, only the ones in the main body of the table.

11. Use any method to add a new row to the table. The simplest is to select the bottom-right cell and press Tab.

12. Enter a new row of data.

13. The formula will update to include the new number in the sum.

Your Average Function

SUM is not the only function that works well in a footer row. You can also use AVERAGE, MAXIMUM, MINIMUM, and PRODUCT.

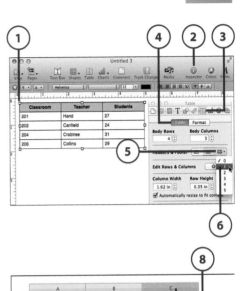

Classroom	Teacher	Students
201	Hand	27
202	Canfield	24
204	Crabtree	31
206	Collins	29
		=SUM(Students)

Classroom	Teacher	Students
201	Hand	27
202	Canfield	24
204	Crabtree	31
206	Collins	29
		111

Classroom	Teacher	Students
201	Hand	27
202	Canfield	24
204	Crabtree	31
206	Collins	29
208	Beadle	18
		129

Table Cell Formatting

One other basic thing you may want to do with cells in tables is to set them to the proper format. For instance, you may want dates to appear a certain way, and prices to appear formatted as money.

1. Create a sample table like this one.

2. Bring up the Inspector window.

3. Go to the Table inspector.

4. Click Format.

5. Select all the cells of the first column.

6. Choose the format type Date and Time.

7. Choose a format for the date.

8. Choose a format for the time (if you just want to show the date in the cells, choose None).

9. Choose all the cells in the third column.

10. Set the format to Currency.

11. In this case, the defaults for currency are fine, but you may want to further customize the currency symbol and other factors.

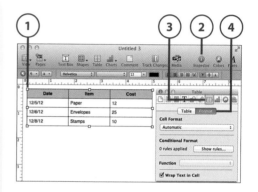

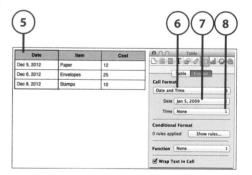

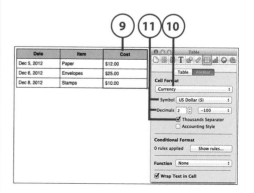

On One Condition

You can also make formatting conditional. Click the Show Rules button in the Conditional Format section of the Table inspector to start the process. You can define a format that will only appear if a condition is met. For instance, if a number in a cell is negative, it can appear red. Or if a number is greater than that of a number in another cell, it can be bold.

Creating charts

Entering chart data

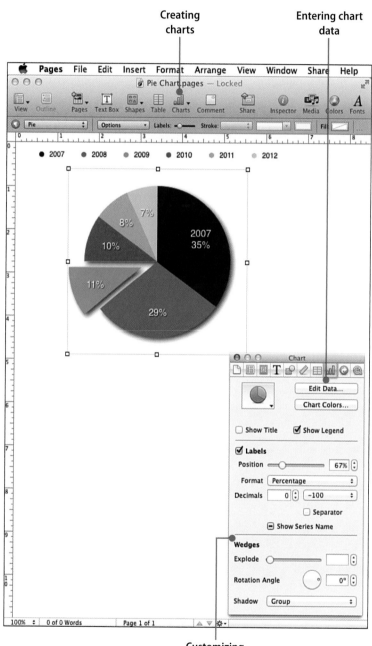

Customizing charts

Creating Charts

If you need something more visual than a table full of data, you can use charts. There are several kinds of charts, such as bar graphs, line graphs, and pie charts. You've also got a plethora of chart colors and styles, including customizable 3D graphics.

Creating a Basic Bar Graph

Although the different types of charts may vary greatly in appearance, the underlying controls are very similar. Therefore, learning how to make a basic bar graph will teach you what you need to know to create other charts.

Pages calls vertical bar graphs *column charts* and horizontal bar graphs *bar charts*. We'll create a vertical column chart, but the same technique can be used to create a horizontal one.

1. Create a new document. Charts work in both word processing and page layout documents, but we use a page layout document in this example.

2. Click the Charts button on the toolbar.

3. Select the first type of chart, called a column chart.

4. You should see a sample chart. Instead of starting with a blank chart, like you do with with tables, you'll always get sample data when starting a new chart so that you have something to start with.

5. The Chart Data Editor should also appear as a separate window. If it does not, you can choose Format, Chart, Show Data Editor.

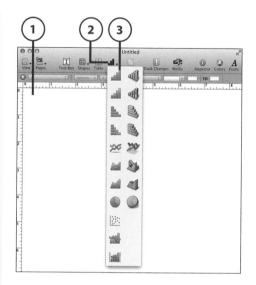

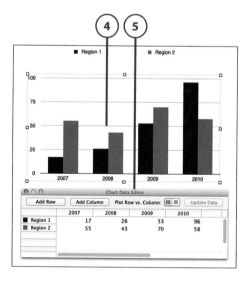

6. To add another item to the chart, click the Add Column button.

7. Add a label for that item by double-clicking the header cell in the table.

8. Add data for that item.

9. You'll see a new item appear in real time as you use the Chart Data Editor.

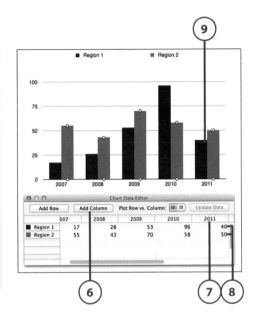

Charts Linked to Numbers

Another way to create a chart is to build it first in Numbers, Apple's spreadsheet app. You can create a chart there and then copy and paste it into your Pages document. The difference would be that the Numbers-created chart would be linked to data in the Numbers spreadsheet.

Then you can update the values in the spreadsheet and use the Update Data button in the Chart Data Editor in Pages to bring in the new values.

Customizing Charts

After you have a chart, you can customize its colors and other visual attributes. You can choose from various sets of colors. You can add or remove labels and titles from the chart.

Modifying 2D Charts

Charts can be divided into two types: 2D and 3D. The difference is only visual. Both chart types represent the same information.

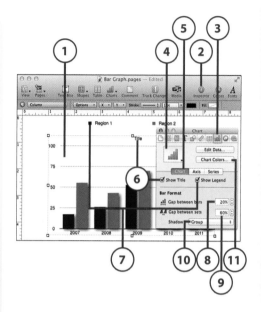

1. Select the chart.

2. Bring up the Inspector window.

3. Select the Chart inspector.

4. Even after you have created the chart and added values, you can still change the basic chart type to something else.

5. Click Chart.

6. Select Show Title to have a small title text box appear above the chart. You can double-click the text box to edit it.

7. Show Legend will add text boxes for each row in the chart's data set.

8. You can adjust the gap between the bars in each set.

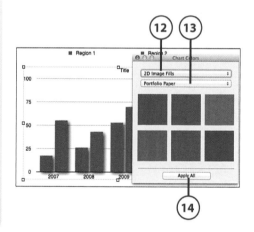

9. You can also adjust the gap between sets of bars.

10. You can add a shadow under the bars.

11. Click Chart Colors.

12. Choose a basic color category.

13. Choose a color subcategory.

14. Click the Apply All button to apply the color selection to the chart.

Drag and Drop Colors

Instead of clicking the Apply All button, you can drag and drop any color in the Chart Colors window onto an element of your chart. This way, you can specify exactly which colors are used for which series, and even mix and match colors from different categories.

Modifying 3D Charts

If you want your charts to visually jump off the page, switch to using a 3D chart. Most chart types have 2D and 3D versions, so switching is easy.

1. In the Chart inspector, click to select a new chart type.

2. Select one of the 3D chart types on the right side.

3. The chart will now appear in 3D.

4. Set the chart colors.

5. A special 3D Chart adjustment control will appear in its own window and in the Inspector. Click and drag inside this control to rotate the chart in its 3D space.

6. Try different lighting styles to see which one you like best.

7. Set the depth of the bars in the chart.

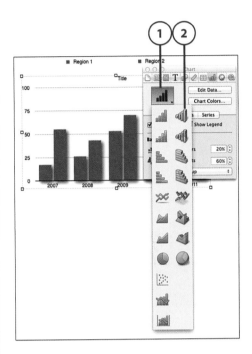

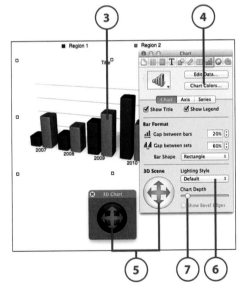

Creating Line Graphs

If line graphs are what you need, you can create them in the same way as bar graphs. Line graphs do not have as many chart options because there are no bars to space or put shadows under. However, they have the same Axis options as bar graphs, so let's create a line graph and use it to learn about that part of the Chart inspector.

1. Start a new page layout document.

2. Click the Charts button on the toolbar.

3. Click the Line Graph option.

4. A line graph will appear with sample data. You use the same Chart Data Editor to change the values as you did with a bar graph.

5. Bring up the Inspector window.

6. Go to the Chart inspector.

7. Click Axis.

8. We'll start by setting some options for the Y axis. These are the same for the X axis.

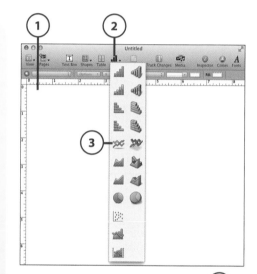

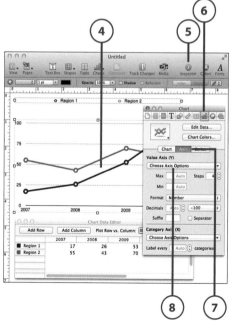

9. The pull-down menu provides a series of options you can select to turn on or off. You can decide whether elements such as a line for the axis, a line all the way around the chart, or the title, are shown at all.

10. You can choose whether values are shown on the Y axis.

11. You can also add tick marks. This set of items allows you to choose one of four options: no tick marks, inside tick marks, centered tick marks, and outside tick marks. Try each one to see how it looks with your particular graph.

12. You can also turn on or off gridlines in your graph.

13. You can set the number of steps in the Y axis. For instance, when Steps was set to 4, the Y axis had four steps: 25, 50, 75, 100. Now that Steps is set to 5, the steps are 20, 40, 60, 80, and 100.

14. You can change the format of the numbers (for instance, choosing currency instead of plain numbers).

15. You can specify the number of decimal places shown.

16. You can choose how negative numbers are represented, with either a minus sign or in parentheses.

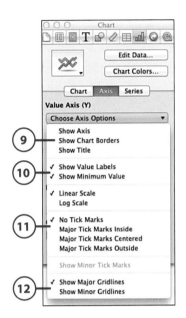

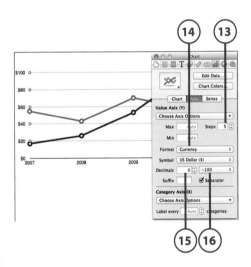

17. Switch to the Series section of the Chart inspector.

18. You can choose a different symbol for each point.

19. You can switch to a curve rather than a straight line between points.

20. Turn on Value Labels to have each point labeled with its value.

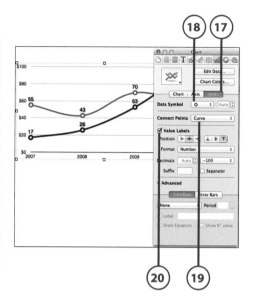

Apply Selectively

You don't need to apply style changes to your entire chart. You can select a single series and change just the properties for that series. This way, you could have one series with straight lines and another with curved lines.

Creating Pie Charts

The third major type of chart is the pie chart. Pages allows you create 2D or 3D pie charts. You can make simple ones, or use colors and textures to create what almost seem like physical objects. Pie charts are great for taking a whole amount, like a budget or population, and visually showing the divisions within it.

1. Open a blank page layout document.

2. Click the Charts button on the toolbar.

3. Select the 2D pie chart.

4. You get a basic pie chart in the middle of your page.

5. Use the same Chart Data Editor to change the values in the chart.

6. Pie charts only use the first row of data.

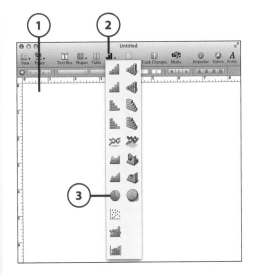

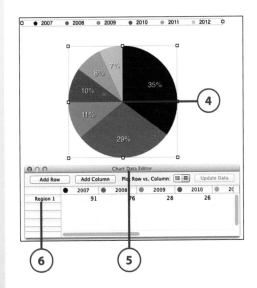

7. Bring up the Inspector window.

8. Go to the Chart inspector.

9. You can remove or alter the appearance of the labels. The Position setting determines how far from the center of the pie the label appears.

10. You can add the column names for each item in the pie chart.

11. Choose only one slice of the pie by clicking it.

12. Move that slice away from the center of the pie to emphasize it.

13. Add a shadow under just that slice, or the entire pie chart.

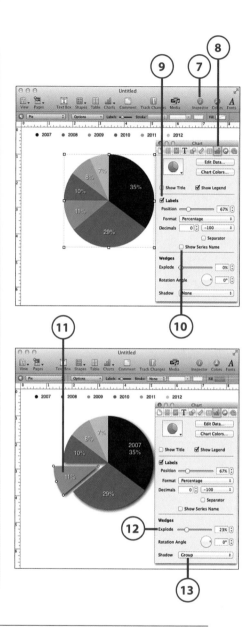

Duplicate and Test

So many visual options are associated with a pie chart that you may want to experiment to get the look that fits best with your document. You can choose Edit, Duplicate with the chart selected to get a second copy of it and then experiment with that copy. If you don't like where you end up, you can delete it and start afresh with a new copy.

Adding audio
and video

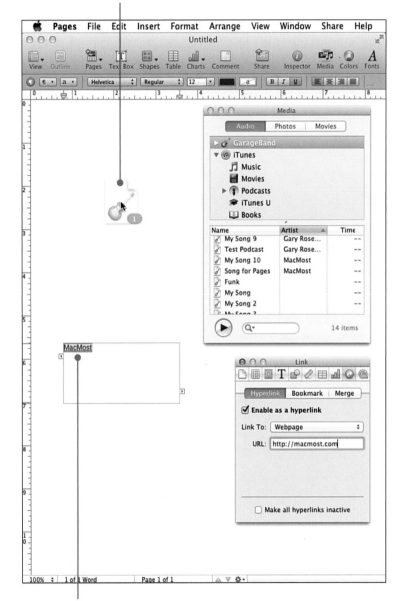

Adding hyperlinks
and bookmarks

In this chapter, you'll learn how to add special elements to your documents, including:

→ Adding web links
→ Adding links inside your document
→ Adding audio to your document
→ Adding video to your document

Adding Links and Media

In addition to photographs and clipart, you can also add audio and video to your Pages documents. Naturally, those can only be played back by someone viewing your document in electronic format.

Another thing you can have in electronic formats is links. If you need to refer to a web page, you can insert a clickable link. Links can also be used to let the reader jump from page to page in your document.

Adding Web Links

If you plan on distributing your document as a file, you can add clickable links. Making any word in your document clickable is done using the Inspector.

1. Select a word or words in your document that will become the linked text.

2. Bring up the Inspector window.

3. Go to the Link inspector.

4. Click Hyperlink.

5. Turn on Enable as a Hyperlink.

6. Set the link to go to a web page by selecting the Webpage option.

7. Enter the full URL, starting with **http://**, for the web page address.

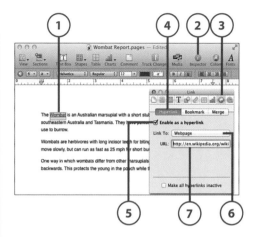

Links Work Everywhere

A link in your Pages document will work when exported to almost any electronic format: PDF, Word, Rich Text, and ePub. Links won't work in plain-text documents and, of course, on printed paper.

Email Links

Instead of Webpage, you can also choose Email Message in step 6. Then you can enter in a destination email address and a subject line. When the reader clicks this link, his default email application will launch and start a new message with that recipient and subject. This depends on the reader's having an email application (some people use only web-based email). The reader then has to compose a message and send it. This kind of link is useful for giving the reader a way to contact you from inside the document.

Adding Links Inside Your Document

Bookmarks are links inside your document. You can give the reader a chance to click some text and jump instantly to another page in your document.

1. Set the destination for the bookmark by selecting some text in your document.

2. Bring up the Inspector window.

3. Go to the Link inspector.

4. Click Bookmark.

5. Click the + button to add the selected text to the list of bookmarks in the document.

6. You'll see the text and the page added to the list. Now you have a destination set for the bookmark link.

7. Select the text in your document that should link to the bookmark.

8. Click Hyperlink in the Link inspector.

9. Enable the text as a hyperlink.

10. Select Bookmark.

11. Choose from the list of bookmarks.

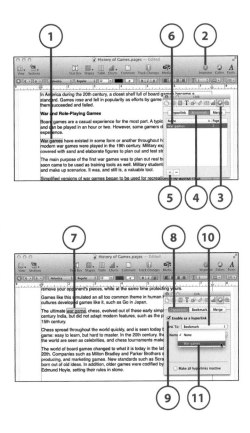

>>>Go Further

BOOKMARKS WORK IN LIMITED SITUATIONS

It appears that links to bookmarks work only if you are viewing the document in Pages. In the author's tests, the bookmarked links appeared in PDF viewers and Word, but could not be relied on to work as a way to jump to another part of the document.

Furthermore, bookmarks only work in word processing documents. They do not operate in page layout documents.

Link to Another Pages Document

A fourth type of link is one that takes the reader to another Pages document. Select this type and you will be prompted to locate a file that will open when the reader clicks the link.

Adding Audio to Your Document

Adding audio to a document has limited application because it can only be used when the reader is running Pages or Word. (The same goes for adding video.) Provided this is true, however, you can create rich multimedia documents. This could prove useful in school reports, when gathering research, and when producing study guides or in-house training manuals.

1. Start a new document.

2. Bring up the Media window.

3. Choose Audio.

4. Browse through your GarageBand and iTunes collections to select your Music library. You can also select a playlist.

5. Use the search box to narrow down your list even more to find the audio you want to import.

6. Select the audio file.

7. Use the play button to preview it.

8. Drag the selection from the Media window into your document.

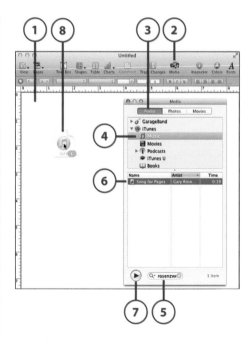

9. The audio appears as a white speaker icon in your document. You can drag it to position it on the page.

10. Bring up the Inspector window.

11. Go to the QuickTime inspector.

12. You can set a specific start and end point for the audio if you don't want the whole thing to play.

13. You can set the audio to repeat or loop.

14. You can adjust the volume for the audio.

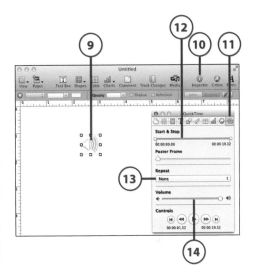

Audio in Action

When readers see the audio file, they just click it and it will play. Because this isn't obvious, you might want to put your own text near the icon to let readers know it is a clickable element.

Move It Like an Image

You can move the audio icon around like an image. So, you can put it inside a shape, stretch it to resize the icon, and even use Object Causes Wrap to have text wrap around it.

Works in Word

If you export to a Word file, the audio will be converted to an audio-only QuickTime file and placed in a subfolder. The audio appears and can be clicked to play in the Word document, although a Windows user would need to have QuickTime installed for it to work.

Adding Video to Your Document

Adding video works pretty much the same way as adding audio. However, because video has a visual element, there is a little more you can do with it.

1. Start a new document.

2. Bring up the Media window.

3. Choose Movies.

4. Browse through your iPhoto and iMovie collections to select your Photos library. You can also select an album or other grouping.

5. Use the search box to narrow down your list even more to find the video you want to import.

6. Select the video file.

7. Use the play button to preview it.

8. Drag the selection from the Media window into your document.

9. The video appears as a rectangle showing a single frame of the video in your document. You can drag it to position it on the page.

10. Bring up the Inspector window.

11. Go to the QuickTime inspector.

12. You can set a specific start and end point for the video if you don't want the whole thing to play.

13. You can use the Poster Frame slider to choose which frame of the video represents it in the document before it has been played.

14. You can set the video to repeat or loop.

15. You can adjust the volume for the audio.

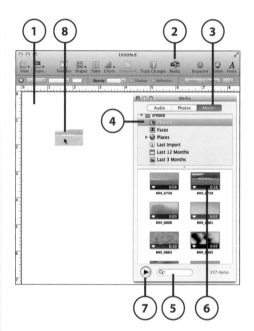

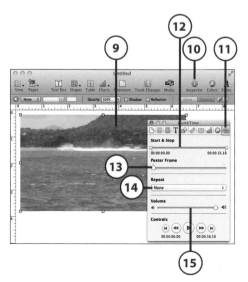

16. When the video is selected, use any of the corner or side handles to resize it.

17. Go to the Graphic inspector.

18. You can set a border for the video. You can use any of the line or picture frame borders as if the video were a still image.

19. You can also set a shadow under the video in the same way you would for an image.

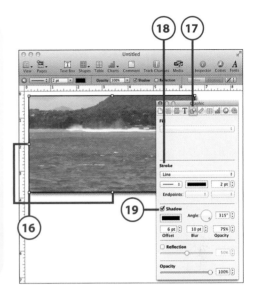

Lights, Camera, Action!

When the reader sees the video file, he or she just clicks it and it will play. It is up to you and the author of the document to let the reader know this is possible. A bit of text under the video would work. Alternatively, the video could be produced with a play button on the first frame so that the reader naturally clicks it.

Works in Word

If you export the video to a Word file, it is converted to a QuickTime movie and placed in a subfolder. Thus, it appears in the Word document just as it does in the Pages document. However, a Windows user would need to have QuickTime installed for the video to work.

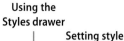

Using the
Styles drawer

Setting style
properties

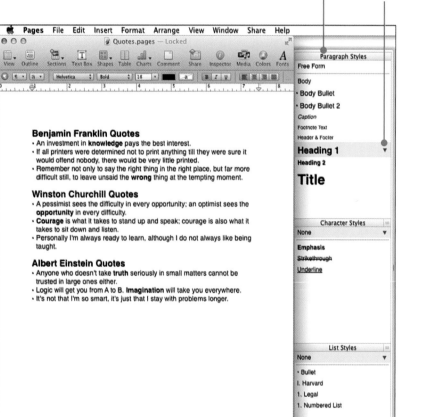

In this chapter, you'll learn about using styles in Pages, including:

- → Using existing styles
- → Modifying an existing style
- → Using character styles
- → Saving styles in documents
- → Copying and pasting styles

Creating and Using Styles

In Chapter 3, "Typing, Selecting, and Manipulating Text," we looked at selecting fonts, changing the font size, and styling text. Although you can customize any line, word, or character in your document, it can get tedious to select the same options for similar elements throughout your document.

For instance, if you wanted to change every section heading from 18-point bold italic text to 24-point bold text, you would have to set the size and font attributes every time. Then if you decided to change it back to 18-point bold italic, you'd need to go back to every heading and make the necessary changes again.

Instead, you can use styles. A style is a saved set of text properties, such as font face, size, line height, and so on. By assigning a style to a line of text, you make it easy to repeat the use of that style. And you can change the options for that style throughout your document.

Using Existing Styles

Every Pages document starts with a set of default styles. You can access and use them with the Styles Drawer.

1. Start off with a document that is relatively plain, with no styles applied, like the one shown here. Use the word processing Blank template.

2. Choose View, Show/Hide Styles Drawer to open the Styles Drawer. You can use Shift-⌘-T as well.

3. The Styles Drawer will appear either to the right or the left of the document window, depending on where you have space.

4. The Styles Drawer is divided into three sections: Paragraph Styles, Character Styles, and List Styles.

5. You can use these two buttons to hide the Character Styles and List Styles sections if you do not plan to use them.

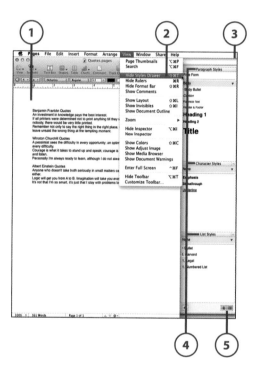

TOC Styles

There is actually a fourth type of style section: Table of Contents Styles. However, you will only see this section in the Styles Drawer if you are currently working on the table of contents for your document.

6. Select the title of the first section. You can select it or simply place your text cursor anywhere in the line.

7. Click the Heading 1 style. The change is applied to the line. It is now larger and bold.

8. Repeat steps 6 and 7 with the other two section titles.

9. Select all the text in the first section.

10. Click the Body Bullet style.

11. Repeat steps 9 and 10 for the next two sections.

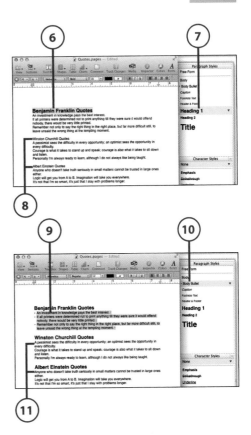

TEMPLATE STYLES

>>>Go Further

When you start a new document with a template, you'll get a different set of styles in the Styles Drawer that come with the template. For instance, choose the Informal Newsletter template and you'll see various Headline, Caption, and Masthead styles. Choose the Real Estate Postcard template and you'll find styles such as Address Label, Logo, Subtitle, and Captions. The Syllabus template has styles such as Calendar and Reading List Reference.

Modifying an Existing Style

Now suppose you don't like the look of a style and you want to change it, but you've already used that style throughout your document. You can change the style and have that change reflected throughout your text.

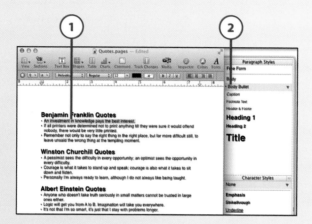

1. Start with the example from the previous task and select some text at the beginning of the first section.

2. Notice that the Styles Drawer shows that the selection uses the Body Bullet style.

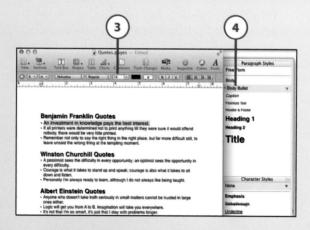

3. Change the font size of the selection. It is now 14 point, when it was previously 12.

4. Notice that a red triangle marker now appears next to the style in the Styles Drawer. This indicates that the selection has been set to that style, but has been modified afterward. Click that triangle.

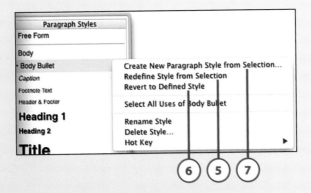

5. To apply the change to all text using that style, select Redefine Style from Selection. This changes all section text in our example to 14 point.

6. Alternatively, you can choose Revert to Defined Style to reset the selection to use the original style and forget your changes.

7. You can also create a new style from any selected text. In addition to this selection here, you can use the + button at the bottom of the Styles Drawer.

Creating New Styles

The difference between redefining a style and creating a new one is simply that you would have a new style added to the Styles Drawer in the second case. You can do this by choosing Create a New Paragraph Style from Selection in step 7, clicking the + button at the bottom of the Styles Drawer, or choosing Create New Paragraph Style from Selection in the Format menu. All of these will let you name the new style and then use the current selection to define the attributes of the style.

Hot Keys

Notice the option to set a "hot key" for a style. You can use the keys F1 to F8 for this. On most Mac keyboards, the F keys are also function keys that perform tasks such as changing the screen brightness or sound volume. You can set this preference in System Preferences, Keyboard with the setting Use All F1, F2, etc. Keys as Standard Function Keys. To get the opposite functionality from this setting, just hold down the Fn key on your keyboard when pressing the F key you want to use.

Using Character Styles

Character styles work just like paragraph styles with one major exception: They do not need to be applied to an entire paragraph. You can apply them to groups of words, a single word, or even a single character.

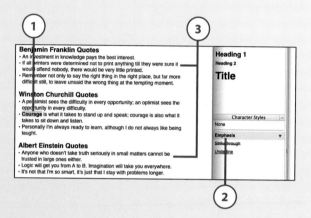

1. Choose a word in your document.

2. Click the Emphasis character style. This makes the word bold.

3. Apply the same style to other words in your text.

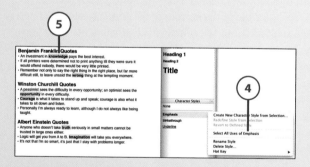

4. Click the triangle next to the Emphasis style and choose Select All Uses of Emphasis. Alternatively, you can just manually select any word that uses this style.

5. Anything that you may have applied that style to will be selected.

6. You can now use steps 3, 4, and 5 from the previous task, "Modifying an Existing Style," to make a change that affects that style everywhere.

Style Type Differences

Certain properties can be used in only one type of style or another. For instance, paragraph styles and not character styles will save line spacing and indentations. Because these properties apply to paragraphs, this makes sense.

Saving Styles in Documents

When you save a document, you are also saving the styles you are using in that document. They are saved in the same file.

Pages has the ability to import styles from another document. So imagine that you create a report for work and you customize the styles in the Styles Drawer for that document. Then, when you start writing a second report, you can import those styles from the first report so that you don't need to re-create them.

You can also create sample documents simply to be used as repositories for styles. Thus, if you plan on creating custom styles to use in a monthly report, you can make a sample report with the styles in it and then import the styles from that sample document each time you start a new report.

1. Create some sample text in a blank word processing document. Try to create some sample text for each part of the document.

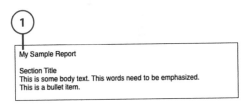

2. Style each section of the document. In this case, separate fonts, styles, and colors are used for the report title, section title, body text, emphasized characters, and bullet items.

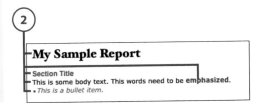

3. Bring up the Styles Drawer by choosing View, Show Styles Drawer or Shift-⌘-T.

4. Select the title.

5. Hover your mouse cursor over the right side of the Styles Drawer directly to the right of the Title style. You should see a small black triangle appear. Click it to bring up this menu.

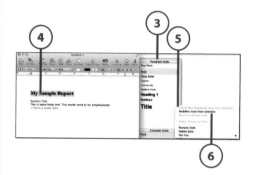

6. Select Redefine Style from Selection. This sets the Title style to the style choices you have made for the sample document.

7. Repeat steps 4 through 6, but this time for the section title and the Heading 1 style.

8. Repeat steps 4 through 6, but this time for the body text and the Body style.

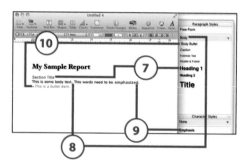

9. Repeat steps 4 through 6, but this time for the emphasized word and the Emphasis style.

10. Repeat steps 4 through 6, but this time for the bullet item and the Body Bullet style.

11. Let's rename the Heading 1 style. Move the mouse cursor to the right of the style name and click the triangle to reveal the menu.

12. Select Rename Style.

13. The style name will become editable. Type **Section Title** to rename it.

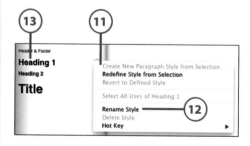

Styles Are for Documents

Note that when you create or set a style, it applies to the document you are working on. If you happen to have a style by that same name in another document, the change doesn't occur there, only in the document you are currently editing.

14. You might want to delete leftover styles you won't be using in your documents. Move the mouse cursor to the right of the Caption style and click the triangle to reveal the menu.

15. Choose Delete Style to remove it. Repeat this for all other unused styles. This step is optional, but it will help you see which styles you have defined in your sample document.

16. Save your document as **Report Styles.pages**.

17. Start a new blank document.

18. Choose Format, Import Styles. Then select your Report Styles. pages document.

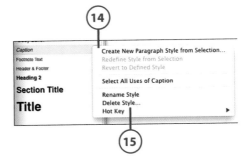

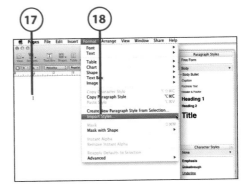

19. You will be prompted with a list of all styles in the document and can make choices about which styles to import. To make things simple in a case like this, choose Select All.

Just One Style for Now

This same technique can be used to simply import one style—for instance, if you are creating a newsletter and you want to use a caption style that you previously used in another document. You can opt to simply import that one style from that older document.

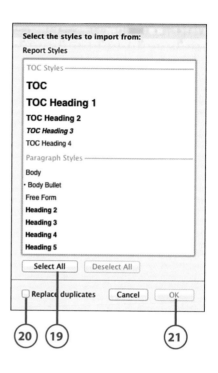

20. Turn on Replace Duplicates. This will replace your new document's styles with the ones from the document you are importing.

21. Click OK. This brings in all the styles from your Report Styles. pages document and replaces the ones you have in your new document with them.

Template Styles Instead

This technique is useful for storing styles to be used in documents later, but in many cases you will want to create a template document instead. We'll look at templates in Chapter 15, "Templates."

Copying and Pasting Styles

Suppose you have stylized a piece of text and you want to reuse that exact style elsewhere. You could create a custom style based on that text, but if you don't want to go that far and just want a one-time duplication of that style, there is an easy way.

1. The word selected here has been colored, bolded, italicized, and enlarged, and it uses a different font.

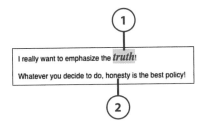

2. You want to make this second word look exactly the same.

3. With the first word still selected, choose Format, Copy Character Style.

4. Select the other word.

5. Choose Format, Paste Character Style. This copies the color, style, size, and font onto the selected word to match the first word. You can paste the style to as many selections as you want.

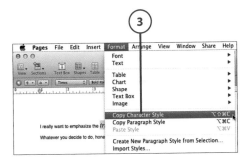

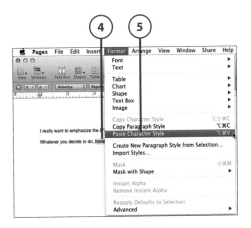

Paragraph Styles, Too

You can use Format, Copy/Paste Paragraph Style to do the same thing with an entire paragraph, including spacing and indentations. You can also copy and paste styles between documents.

Creating a table of contents

Adding headers and footers

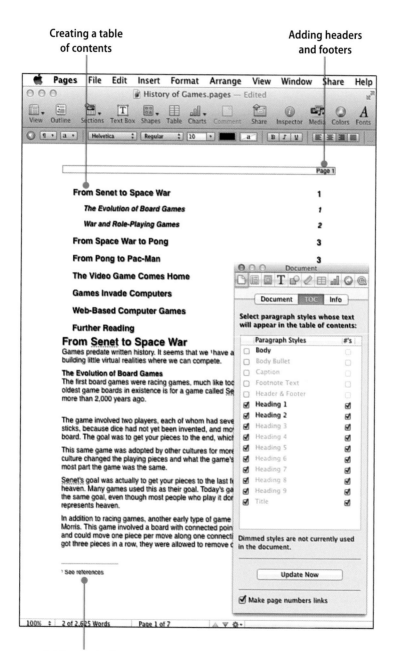

Adding footnotes

In this chapter, you'll learn how to add organizational elements to your documents, including:

→ Creating a table of contents
→ Dividing your document into sections
→ Adding page headers
→ Adding page footers
→ Adding page numbers
→ Building complex headers and footers
→ Adding footnotes and endnotes

Organizing Your Document

Pages includes several ways to help you organize your document. Some of these methods, such as using the table of contents, allow you to provide organization for the reader to use. Other techniques, such as using outlines and page thumbnails, let you as the writer organize while creating the document.

In addition to adding a table of contents, we'll look at adding footnotes and endnotes to your document, two elements that are important for school and business reports.

Creating a Table of Contents

Pages lets you create a table of contents by taking the styles from your document and interpreting them as chapters and subsections. Anything defined as a Heading 1 style, for instance, will be thought of as a section to be mentioned in the table of contents.

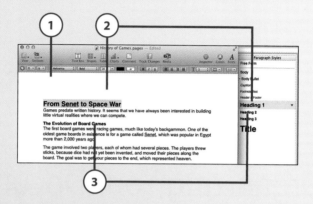

1. Start with a document that has sections.

2. Open the style drawer and set the style of each chapter title to Heading 1.

3. You can also style subsections with Header 2 and so on.

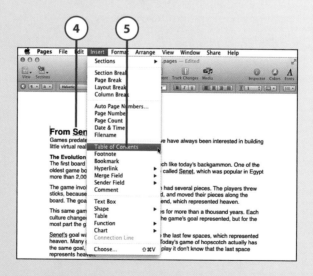

4. Position the text cursor at the very start of the document, or wherever you want the table of contents to appear.

5. Choose Insert, Table of Contents.

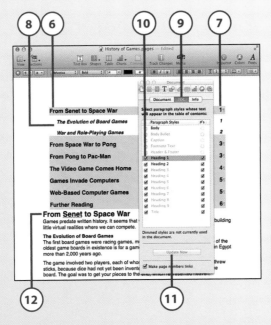

6. The table of contents will appear.

7. Page numbers will appear on the right.

8. This document has seven chapters, plus two subsections to Chapter 1.

9. The Inspector window should open automatically to the Document inspector, TOC section.

10. You can see which styles are used in the table of contents. You can check or uncheck styles to adjust what will be used.

11. As you edit and add to your document, you can always return to this section of the Inspector window and click the Update Now button to re-create the table of contents.

12. Place the text cursor at the end of the table of contents and choose Insert, Page Break to start the text on a fresh new page.

Styling the Table of Contents

You cannot edit the text in the table of contents because it is taken directly from the headings in the main body of your text. However, you can select the text by indentation level and change the style of the fonts used. In fact, there are specific styles named TOC Heading 1 and so on.

Dividing Your Document into Sections

If you are create a large document, you might want to break it up into sections. These sections can be parts of a research paper, such as the abstract, introduction, methods, results, discussion, and citations. Alternatively, they can be parts of a book, such as the introduction, preface, chapters, and epilogue.

Sections are parts of word processing document. They let you break up the document into areas that can be moved around and have different properties. For page layout documents, each page can be thought of as its own section.

1. With a document open, choose View, Page Thumbnails to bring up the page thumbnails on the left side of your document window.

2. Each page in your document is now shown on the left. You can click a page to jump to it.

3. Place the text cursor at the end of a section.

4. Choose Insert, Section Break.

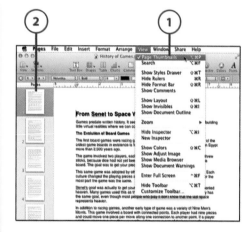

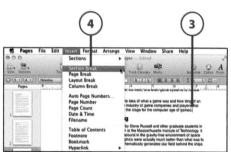

5. The section break also acts as a page break, with the new section starting at the top of a page.

6. When you select a page in the page thumbnails list, a yellow border shows the section. You can now drag and drop whole sections around in your document.

7. Bring up the Inspector window.

8. Choose the Layout inspector.

9. Click Section.

10. You can have page numbering for a section start back at 1 (or any number you choose).

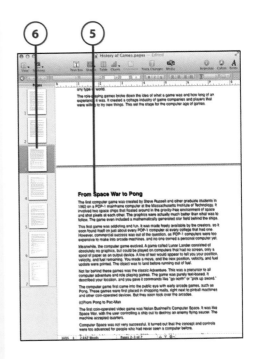

Adding New Sections

To add a new section, you can simply start creating that section at the end of the previous one and then use Insert, Section Break to separate it from the first. Alternatively, you can choose Insert, Sections, Text Page or Blank to create a new page that is in its own new section.

In fact, sometimes it may be useful to have a section that is just a blank page. The purpose of creating a section with a blank page is to have a blank page-layout page in the middle of a word processing document, perhaps for an illustration or aside.

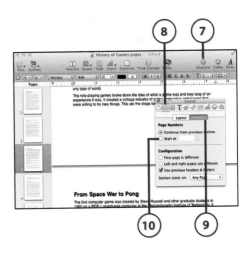

Adding Page Headers

Page headers appear on the pages of word processing documents by default. However, it is up to you to put something in them. The text you enter into a header will appear on every page of your document.

1. To make it easier to see where the header is located, choose View, Show Layout.

2. Bring up the Inspector window.

3. Go to the Document inspector.

4. Click Document.

5. Turn on or off headers by clicking the check box.

6. Set the vertical position of the header.

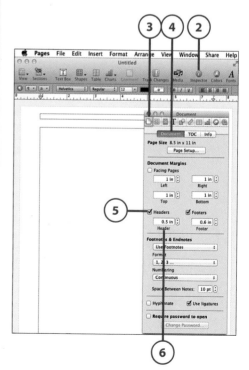

7. Click in the header box and type some text.

8. Check to make sure there is a tab stop at the right side of the ruler; it should be a right tab stop. If not, add it. See "Adding Tab Stops" in Chapter 4, "Styling and Formatting Text."

9. Press the Tab key to move the text cursor to the tab you just created. Then type some text to appear on the right side of the header.

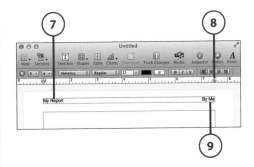

Headers and Tabs

Using tab stops is key to creating good headers and footers in your documents. You can use the right tab stop to position text on the right side of the header. You can use the center tab stop to place text in the center. See "Building Complex Headers and Footers," later in this chapter.

Adding Page Footers

You can also use the footer at the bottom of every page. This text will therefore appear at the bottom of every page of your document.

1. Bring up the Inspector window.

2. Go to the Document inspector.

3. Click Document.

4. Turn on or off footers by clicking the check box.

5. Set the vertical position of the footer.

6. Click in the footer and type some text.

7. Click the center button to center the text in the footer. You can also use Tabs like in the "Adding Page Headers" task to place text on the left and right. See "Building Complex Headers and Footers," later in this chapter.

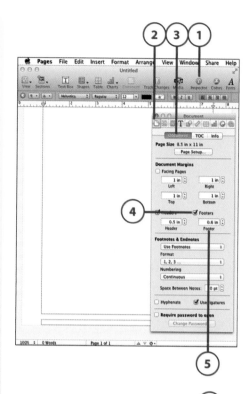

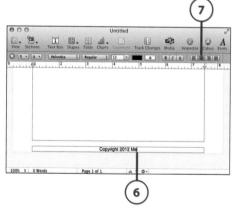

Adding Page Numbers

One of the most common things you will want to do with headers and footers is to add page numbers to your document. In the next section, we look at how to do this manually. Here, we discuss a semi-automatic way to do it, too.

1. Choose Insert, Auto Page Numbers.

2. Choose whether you want the page numbers to appear in the entire document or just this section.

3. You can uncheck this box to start page numbering on the second page, so your first page can be a cover page.

4. Decide whether the page number should appear in the header or footer.

5. Decide whether the page number should be on the left, right, or center. You can also pick inside or outside if your document is set up to be printed on both sides of the paper in book format.

6. Choose the style of numbering. You can use letters instead of numbers. You can even use Roman numerals.

7. This preview area shows the location you have chosen for the page numbers.

8. In this example, the page number appears at the right side of the footer on each page.

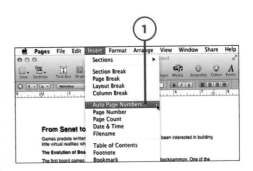

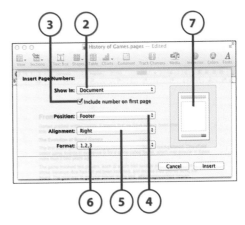

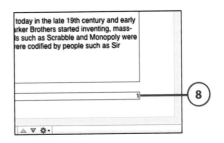

Building Complex Headers and Footers

You can put a lot of different things in headers and footers. Let's build a complex header and footer to demonstrate what you can do.

1. With View, Show Layout turned on, click in the header and type something to appear at the top left.

2. Add a center tab stop. See "Adding Tab Stops" in Chapter 4.

3. Check to make sure the default right tab stop is there at the right side of the ruler.

4. Press Tab to go to the center tab stop.

5. Choose Insert, Date & Time.

Date and Time Format

You can choose from a variety of date and time formats in headers and footers. After you place the date, Control-click it and choose Edit Date & Time. Alternatively, you can double-click the date to bring up the options. You can also Control-click the filename and page numbers to choose the formats of those items.

6. The current date and time are placed in the header. This is not text you can edit, but a special element in the document that contains the current date.

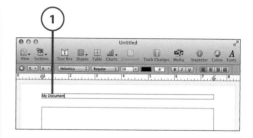

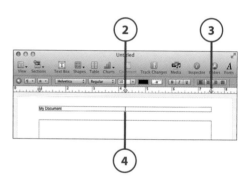

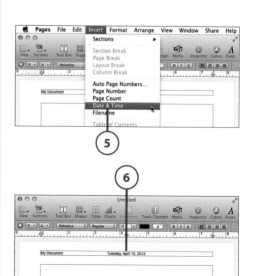

7. Press Tab again to place the cursor up against the right side of the header, where the right tab is located. Anything you add here will be right-justified against the right side.

8. Choose Insert, Filename to place the filename at this location.

9. Click in the footer.

10. Click the center alignment button.

11. Choose Insert, Page Number.

12. Type a space, then the word *of*, and then another space.

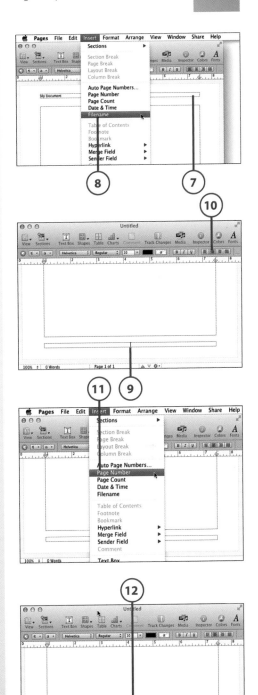

13. Choose Insert, Page Count. This results in a footer that reads something like "1 of 99."

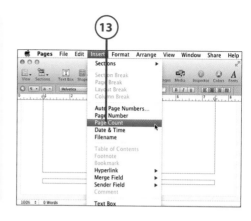

>>>Go Further

NUMBERING SECTIONS INDIVIDUALLY

Suppose you have several sections in your document. Maybe you have some front matter, a table of contents, the main body of text, and then some additional material at the end. If you want, you can make each of these a separate section. Then you can have page numbering start at 1 for each section.

To do this, you need to add page numbers to the header or footer. Then, with your text cursor at the start of each section, access the Layout inspector. Under Page Numbers, set that page to Start At 1. This forces the section to start numbering at page 1, regardless of what number was on the last page of the previous section.

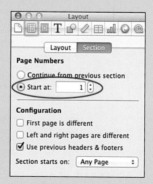

You could also use this in a case where you have a book divided into different documents. If the second document is supposed to start at page 349, you can set page numbering to start at 349 using the Layout inspector.

Adding Footnotes and Endnotes

If you are writing the sort of document that requires footnotes, Pages has you covered. Adding footnotes is easy, and Pages manages them somewhat automatically.

1. Place the text cursor where you want the footnote mark to appear.

2. Choose Insert, Footnote.

3. A footnote symbol appears at the location of the text cursor.

4. A text box with the same footnote symbol appears at the bottom of the page. Add your footnote text here.

5. Go to the Document inspector.

6. You can set your document to use footnotes, section endnotes, or document endnotes.

7. Choose the format for the footnote symbols. For instance, you can switch from regular numbers to Roman numerals.

8. If you are using footnotes, you can set the numbering to be continuous throughout the document, or start at 1 for each page.

9. Set the spacing between footnotes at the bottom of the page.

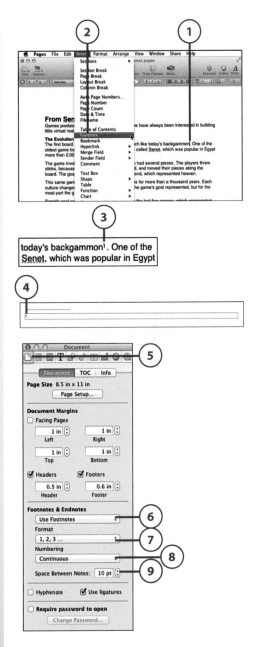

>>>Go Further

FOOTNOTES VERSUS ENDNOTES

Footnotes appear at the bottom of each page. Therefore, the reader only has to look to the bottom of the page to see the contents of the footnote. If you'd rather have the footnotes gathered in one group at the end of the document, then switch to document endnotes. Alternatively, you can use section endnotes to have them grouped at the end of each section, such as each chapter.

Creating your own templates

Using pre-made templates

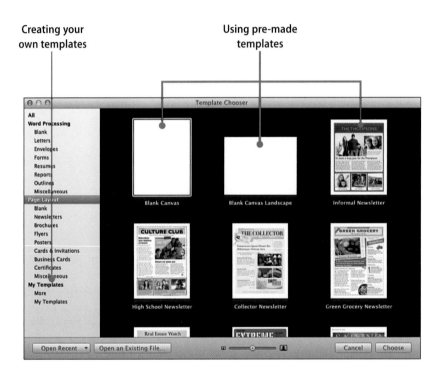

In this chapter, you'll learn how to use templates, including:

→ Exploring pre-made templates
→ Modifying pre-made templates
→ Creating your own template

Using and Building Templates

Pages comes with a large variety of templates that you can use to start your documents. You can also use them to get ideas or dissect them to see how unusual formatting or layouts are done.

In addition, you can modify these templates or create your own. Creating a template can be as simple as saving a sample document or as complex as defining placeholders and different kinds of pages.

Exploring Pre-Made Templates

Before learning how to make your own templates, it is worth looking at some existing templates and examining how they work.

1. Start a new document by choosing File, New. This should bring up the Template Chooser as long as you haven't changed the For New Documents setting in the Pages preferences. Otherwise, you can choose File, New from Template Chooser.

2. Go to Reports in the Word Processing section.

3. Choose the Research Paper template.

4. Click Choose.

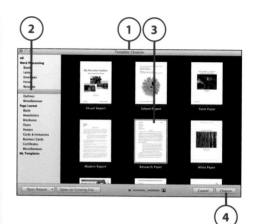

5. A new document is created. Notice how it is already filled with some default text.

6. Some of the text has been filled with custom information, such as your name.

7. Choose View, Show Invisibles. This lets us examine the template closer.

8. By turning on Show Invisibles, we can see boxes around some of the special placeholder text. These fields use your first and last name. In other templates, your address and other information may also be inserted.

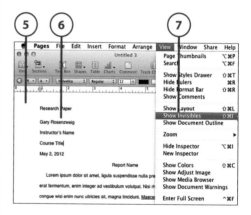

9. There is also other placeholder text, such as these paragraphs filled with Lorem Ipsum text. Clicking in one of these paragraphs will select the entire paragraph and typing will replace it.

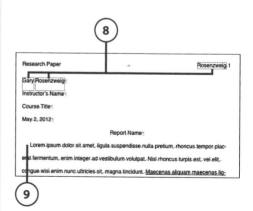

10. Choose Insert, Sections to choose from one of three predefined sections included in the templates. Each template can include its own unique sections. Page layout documents allow you to insert predefined pages instead of predefined sections.

Two Types of Placeholders

There are two types of placeholders: text and media. You can simply select and type to replace the contents of a text placeholder. For media placeholders, you drag and drop images from the Finder or from the Media window into the placeholder. Pasting text and images from the clipboard also works.

Modifying Pre-Made Templates

What if you find a template you like, but it isn't quite perfect? You could modify the document any way you like, of course. However, if this is the type of document you'll be creating often, you might want to create your own variation of that template to use again and again.

1. Start a new document using the Modern Letter template.

2. Leaving everything else alone, let's make some simple changes to the document. Let's change the line style next to the address, and also the logo.

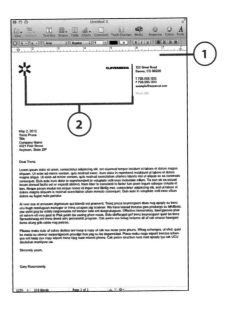

3. Drag and drop a new image into this placeholder area.

4. Select the line and use the format bar to change it to a dotted line.

5. Choose File, Save as Template.

6. You are prompted to save the template in the My Templates folder. You can save it anywhere you like, but templates stored here will appear when you use the Template Chooser.

7. Name the template something you will remember and keep the .template extension.

8. Choose File, New from Template Chooser to bring up the Template Chooser. Click My Templates.

9. You'll see your new template and can choose it.

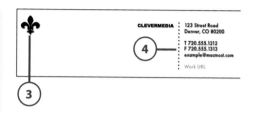

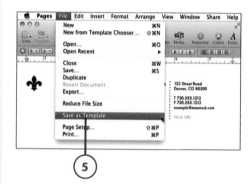

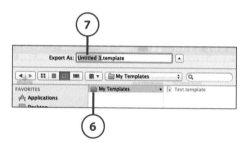

Replace a Template

If you want to update one of your custom templates, simply save the updated version over the old one in the My Templates folder. This will replace it, and you'll only have the new one from that point on.

Delete a Custom Template

The only way to delete a template is to go into your Library folder by switching to the Finder and choosing Go, Library while holding down the Option key. Then go into Application Support/iWork/Pages/ Templates and delete the template file. You can also rename a template by simply renaming the file.

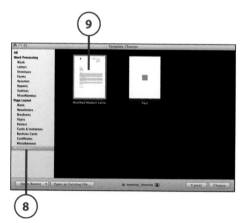

Creating Your Own Template

In addition to making simple modifications to templates, you can create your own from scratch. Actually, you must start with something, so you would start with a blank template and build from there.

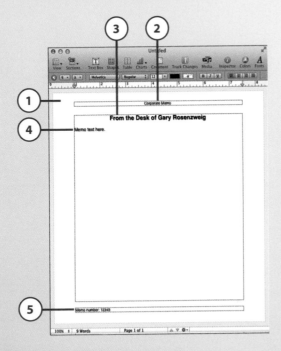

1. Start by creating a document using the Blank word processing template. Choose View, Show Layout so that the borders of the body, header, and footer are visible.

2. Add some text to the header.

3. Add a title to the top of the document. Make it larger, bold, and centered.

4. Add something in place of the body text.

5. Put some text, followed by an identification number, at the bottom in the footer.

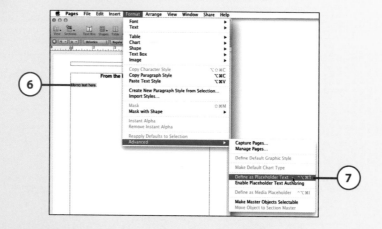

6. Select the body text.

7. Choose Format, Advanced, Define as Placeholder Text. This converts the selected text to placeholder text. When a new document is created with this template, you can select the entire section of text with one click and then replace it by typing.

Get Your Own Lorem Ipsum

The templates that come with Pages use Lorem Ipsum text as placeholder text. If you want to do the same, you can get random Lorem Ipsum text from various websites such as http://www.lipsum.com/.

8. Repeat steps 6 and 7, but select the number 12345 in the footer instead. This turns the number into placeholder text that can easily be selected and replaced.

9. It might be necessary to create several pages in your document that look like this one. Choose Format, Advanced, Capture Pages.

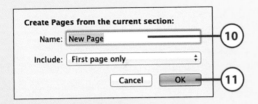

10. Name your new page type.

11. Click OK.

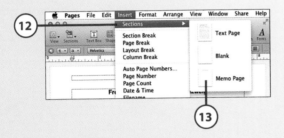

12. Now that you have added a new section type, test it by choosing Insert Sections.

13. A new section type appears based on the page you just captured.

14. Use steps 5–7 from the previous task to save the template after you have made all your changes.

Media Placeholders

If you want an image or graphic in your template, just add any image. Resize it and position it. Then choose Format, Advanced, Define as Media Placeholder. When you use this template later, that image becomes a place where you can drag and drop a new image.

Templates Remember Everything

Before saving your template, you can customize much more than just what you see in the document window. You can use the Inspector to change the document properties, for instance, and that will be remembered in the template you save. Even things such as whether the Styles Drawer is open will be saved.

>>>Go Further

PAGE LAYOUT TEMPLATES

Creating your own templates is a powerful feature of Pages, especially when using page layout documents. Templates work the same way with page layout documents, but the idea of capturing pages becomes even more important. For instance, if you create a newsletter, you can create many varieties of pages with images and text in different locations. Each one can become a section (called simply a "page" in page layout mode), and then you can pick and choose different pages to add to your newsletter each time you create one.

Creating
merge fields

Linking your
documents to data

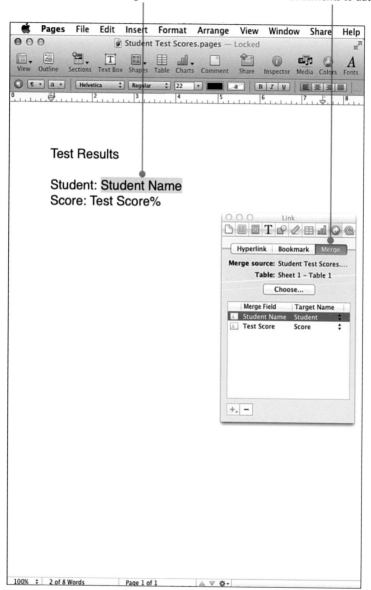

In this chapter, you'll learn about using merges, also known as mail merges, including:

→ Merging contacts with envelopes
→ Merging a spreadsheet with letters
→ Creating your own merge documents

Merges for Letters and Envelopes

There's nothing like adding a personal touch to letters that are not personal at all. If you need to address envelopes and customize letters with the recipient's name, you'll want to learn about Pages' merge feature.

You can take a list of names from your Mac's Contacts app, or from a Numbers spreadsheet, and generate individually addressed envelopes and letters.

Merging Contacts with Envelopes

Let's start with the simplest form of merge: printing out a series of individually addressed envelopes. We'll use one of the templates for this, but later we'll look at how you can create your own.

1. Start a new document with the Template Chooser.

2. Select the Envelopes category.

3. Select the Traditional Envelope template.

4. Click Choose.

5. In the upper-left corner of the envelope will be the return address. You can edit that text if you like.

6. In the middle of the envelope is a placeholder for the recipient's address.

7. Choose Edit, Mail Merge.

8. In the dialog box that appears, select Address Book (Contacts) as the source of your merge data.

9. You can choose a specific group to use, or just all of your contacts.

10. Make sure that you are using the Merge To: Send to Printer option.

11. Click Merge.

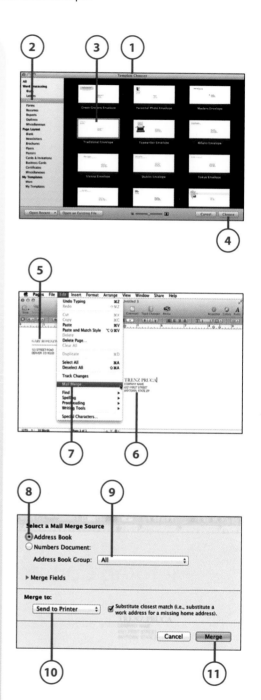

12. A Print dialog will now appear.

13. You can see a preview of one page of your merged document.

14. You can flip through the pages of your document to check it over before printing.

15. Click the Print button to send the document to the printer.

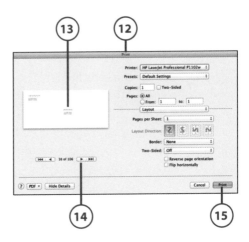

>>>Go Further

CREATING A CONTACTS GROUP

Before using your contacts to create a merge, you should set up a group in your Contacts app (called Address Book in Mac OS X 10.7 Lion and earlier). Chances are you don't want to send a letter to every single person in your contacts, but just a selection of them.

Within Contacts, choose File, New Group. Then drag and drop contacts from the main list onto that group to add them. Click the group to view the list.

Once that is all set, you can return to Pages and create your merge, specifying that group in step 9. You can even preview that merge, cancel instead of printing, and then update your Contacts group and try again. The next time you try, the updated group list will be used.

Merging a Spreadsheet with Letters

Another data source for merges is a spreadsheet created in Apple's spreadsheet app, Numbers. This allows you to compile a list of names, addresses, or other information and merge it into a document, such as an envelope or letter. The result is the same as using your Contacts app, but the way you prepare the source data is different.

1. Start a new document with the Template Chooser.

2. This time let's use a letter document as an example, so click Letters.

3. Select the Green Grocery Letter template.

4. Click Choose.

5. The letter includes the name and address of the recipient. This is the text that will vary from copy to copy using our data.

6. Bring up the Inspector window.

7. Choose the Link inspector.

8. Click Merge.

9. Here we have a list of the merge fields in the document and the target name for each. This name is what we will need to create the Numbers document. Each target name must correspond to a column heading in the spreadsheet.

10. Here is a sample Numbers document that can be used with Pages to create this merge.

11. Notice that the column headings row matches the target names in Pages.

12. Click the Choose button in the Link inspector to change the merge data from your Contacts (Address Book) to a Numbers document.

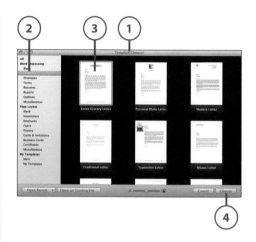

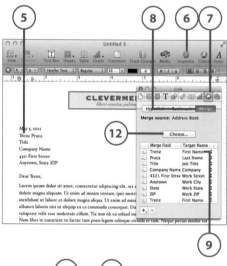

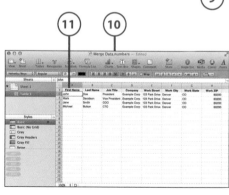

13. Choose Numbers Document.

14. Click the Choose button to open the document you created in Numbers.

15. If your document contains more than one spreadsheet or table, you can choose the proper one.

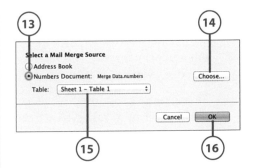

Close, but Not Quite

Once you choose the Numbers document, you can look in the Link inspector to make sure all the columns match the target names. Any targets that are missing will be in red. Often this is simply due to mistyping the column name.

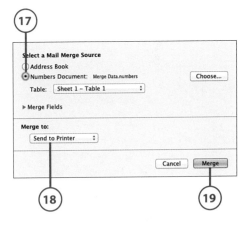

16. Click OK.

17. Choose Edit, Mail Merge. This gives you the same dialog box that you saw in the last task in step 8, but this time the Numbers document is already selected.

18. Make sure you have selected Merge To: Send to Printer.

19. Click Merge.

20. You'll get a Print dialog and can flip through the previews to check your merge before printing.

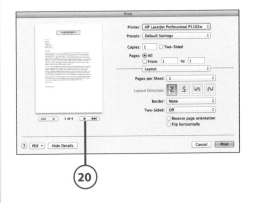

Creating Your Own Merge Documents

Merges can be used for more than just addressing letters and envelopes. You can use them any time you want to compose a single document and then produce variations of it based on data.

As an example, suppose you are a teacher and you need to send home test scores to parents. You have each student's name and score in a Numbers spreadsheet. Now you just need to produce a sheet to send home to each parent.

1. Start with a Numbers spreadsheet that looks like this. In the first column are the student names, and the second column has their scores. Each column has a header cell at the top with the proper name for that column.

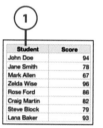

Student	Score
John Doe	94
Jane Smith	78
Mark Allen	67
Zelda Wise	96
Rose Ford	86
Craig Martin	82
Steve Block	79
Lana Baker	93

2. Create a new word processing document in Pages. Put the text shown here in it. No need for any special formatting yet.

3. Bring up the Inspector window.

4. Go to the Link inspector.

5. Click Merge.

6. Click Choose to select a source for the merge.

7. Choose to use a Numbers document for the merge.

8. Select the document you created in step 1.

9. Select the text Student Name in your document. This is the placeholder text you want to replace with the actual student's name.

10. Click the + button in the Inspector window to add the selected text as a merge field. When prompted, choose Add Merge Field.

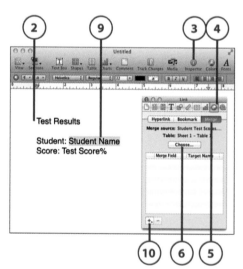

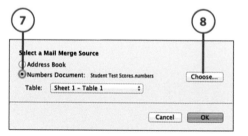

11. Notice that the selected text has been added to the list of merge fields.

12. Click the target for the field and select Student. Notice the list (Student, Score) has been taken from the column headings in our Numbers document.

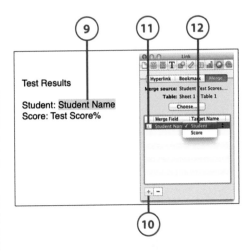

13. Repeat steps 9 to 12 for the text Test Score. Only select Test Score, not the percent symbol. Now you have two merge fields, each linked to one of the two columns in your Numbers document.

14. When you choose Edit, Mail Merge and then Print, you will get a document that replaces the two fields with the data.

15. You can flip through the pages to check them before printing.

16. Click Print to send to the printer.

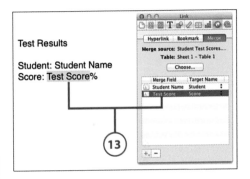

Live Data

When you choose Edit, Mail Merge, you get the latest data from your spreadsheet. Therefore, if you update your Numbers spreadsheet, the next time you perform the merge it will use the updated data cells. In fact, you can have Pages and Numbers open at the same time and update Numbers just before performing the merge.

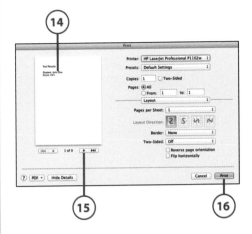

Editing while keeping
track of changes

Reviewing and
accepting edits

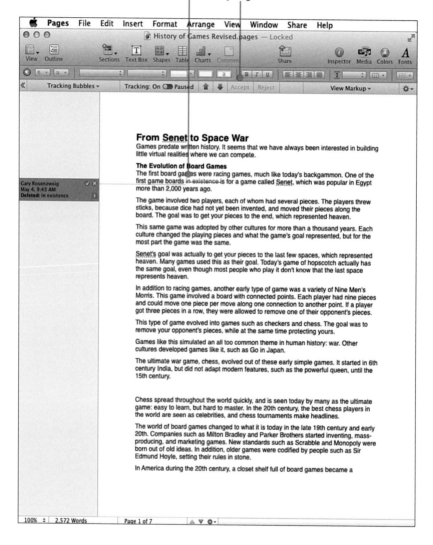

From Senet to Space War
Games predate written history. It seems that we have always been interested in building
little virtual realities where we can compete.

The Evolution of Board Games
The first board games were racing games, much like today's backgammon. One of the
first game boards in existence is for a game called Senet, which was popular in Egypt
more than 2,000 years ago.

The game involved two players, each of whom had several pieces. The players threw
sticks, because dice had not yet been invented, and moved their pieces along the
board. The goal was to get your pieces to the end, which represented heaven.

This same game was adopted by other cultures for more than a thousand years. Each
culture changed the playing pieces and what the game's goal represented, but for the
most part the game was the same.

Senet's goal was actually to get your pieces to the last few spaces, which represented
heaven. Many games used this as their goal. Today's game of hopscotch actually has
the same goal, even though most people who play it don't know that the last space
represents heaven.

In addition to racing games, another early type of game was a variety of Nine Men's
Morris. This game involved a board with connected points. Each player had nine pieces
and could move one piece per move along one connection to another point. If a player
got three pieces in a row, they were allowed to remove one of their opponent's pieces.

This type of game evolved into games such as checkers and chess. The goal was to
remove your opponent's pieces, while at the same time protecting yours.

Games like this simulated an all too common theme in human history: war. Other
cultures developed games like it, such as Go in Japan.

The ultimate war game, chess, evolved out of these early simple games. It started in 6th
century India, but did not adapt modern features, such as the powerful queen, until the
15th century.

Chess spread throughout the world quickly, and is seen today by many as the ultimate
game: easy to learn, but hard to master. In the 20th century, the best chess players in
the world are seen as celebrities, and chess tournaments make headlines.

The world of board games changed to what it is today in the late 19th century and early
20th. Companies such as Milton Bradley and Parker Brothers started inventing, mass-
producing, and marketing games. New standards such as Scrabble and Monopoly were
born out of old ideas. In addition, older games were codified by people such as Sir
Edmund Hoyle, setting their rules in stone.

In America during the 20th century, a closet shelf full of board games became a

In this chapter, you'll learn how to review your documents for editing purposes, including:

→ Adding comments
→ Tracking changes
→ Adding revision marks
→ Reviewing changes

Reviewing Documents

After you have created a document, you may want to edit it. Perhaps you may even want to collaborate with one or more editors on a single document.

Pages lets you add comments to a document as well as track changes as you, or one or more editors, review it. A teacher or classmate working together with you on a project can also leave notes and make changes. Then the author or a lead editor can review the changes and accept or reject them.

Adding Comments

Before we look at using the revision-tracking system in Pages, let's take a look at the simpler commenting system. This lets you add comments to your document that won't appear when it is exported or printed.

1. Select some text in your document that you want to comment on. You can also just place your text cursor at a location to leave a comment for that exact spot.

2. Click the Comment button on the toolbar. You can also choose Insert, Comment.

3. The comments sidebar then appears on the left. You can show and hide the comments sidebar with View, Show/Hide Comments.

4. Your comment appears in the sidebar, prepopulated with your name and the time.

5. The text you had selected will have a yellow box and line that extends to the comment.

6. You can edit the text in the comment just like normal text. In fact, following step 2, the text focus would be on the comment with it all selected, so you can simply start typing to replace the default name and time and enter your comment.

7. If you ever need to delete a comment, simply click the X button in the upper-right corner.

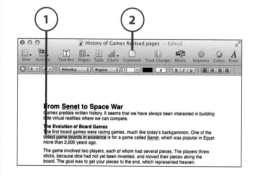

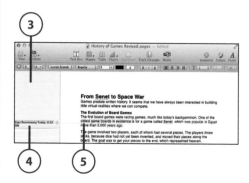

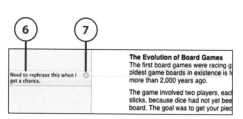

Printing Comments

Printing your documents with comments is just a matter of printing while the comments sidebar is visible. If it is, the comments will be included in the printout. If it is hidden, the comments will not be printed.

Tracking Changes

Using the change-tracking process in Pages can be divided into two major parts. First, there is the addition of revision marks. You can suggest changes to the document without actually making those changes. Second, there is the acceptance or rejection of each change.

Adding Revision Marks

To add revision marks, you simply need to turn on change tracking and then edit your document as you normally would. You can add text, delete text, or modify text. The changes are made, with revision marks, and your original text is still there, as well, in case you want to revert to it.

1. Before you start tracking changes, review your Change Tracking preferences by choosing Pages, Preferences. Under General Preferences, check your name. Your name, as it appears here, will be used to mark any changes you make.

2. This is also where you can define how deleted and inserted text looks when you add revisions.

3. To start tracking changes, choose Edit, Track Changes.

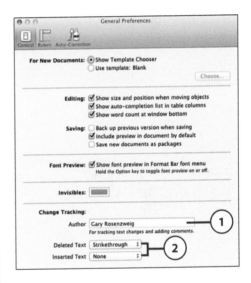

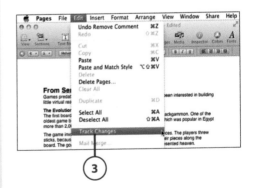

4. The tracking toolbar will appear at the top of the document window. This contains all the controls you need to use change tracking.

5. Click the reveal button at the far left of the toolbar to show or hide the change tracking sidebar you see here on the left.

6. You can temporarily pause change tracking at any time with this switch. While it's paused, you can make normal changes to your text that won't be recorded as edits and won't show up as changes in a future review of the document.

7. To make a change, select some text or place the text cursor in your document as you would normally do to edit it.

8. Type to delete and replace the selected word. The new word appears and the old word remains, but with a line through it.

9. In the sidebar, the details from the revision are shown, including the username, time, and what was done.

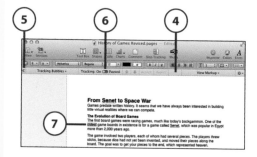

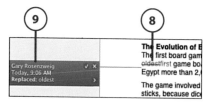

Show Only Some Revisions

The sidebar shows the details of the revisions. These are called tracking bubbles. You can select the Tracking Bubbles pull-down menu on the toolbar and select whether all, none, or only selected revisions are shown in the sidebar. Choosing to see only selected revisions means that only those in the selected area of the text are visible, which could help you examine changes in a crowded area of your document.

You can also use this pull-down menu to decide whether changes that are only formatting changes are shown (for instance, if a word has been bolded or the font size changed).

10. Select words you want to delete and simply press the Delete key on your keyboard. The deleted text now has a line through it.

11. On the left the change is noted.

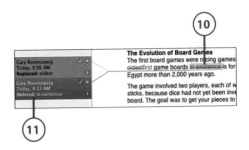

Author Color

If you have several people editing the document, each should get his or her own color. You can set the color being used for changes at any time by clicking the gear-like settings button on the right side of the tracking changes toolbar and then choosing Author Color.

Reviewing Changes

After you have made changes to your document with tracking changes turned on, you have a variety of pending changes you need to review. If others have been editing your document, you'll have even more.

So the next step is to go through the changes and accept or reject them. An accepted change becomes a permanent part of the document.

1. Click the down-arrow button on the toolbar. This takes you to the next suggested revision.

2. The change is highlighted.

3. Click the check mark button to accept the change and make it permanent.

4. Or, click the X button to reject the change and restore the original text.

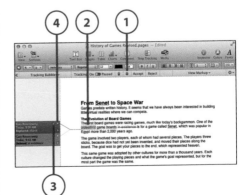

5. The change has been made and is still selected. The revision completely disappears from the left sidebar because the change is now permanent.

6. Repeat step 1 to go to the next revision.

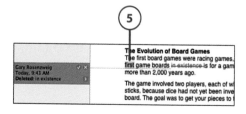

Markup Viewing Choices

The toolbar has a pull-down menu named View Markup that could make it easier for you to review your changes. For instance, you can select to hide all of the prechange text in the document, leaving only the sidebar notes and the lines that link to it. This will help you see and read the final text of the document, assuming you should accept the changes.

Accept All Changes

The gear-like tools pull-down on the far right side of the toolbar has options for accepting or rejecting all changes. This can come in handy if you are editing the document and have carefully reviewed all the changes without accepting them, only rejecting the ones you don't want. Then with one action you can accept the rest. Alternatively, you could accept the ones you want and leave the others and then reject the rest.

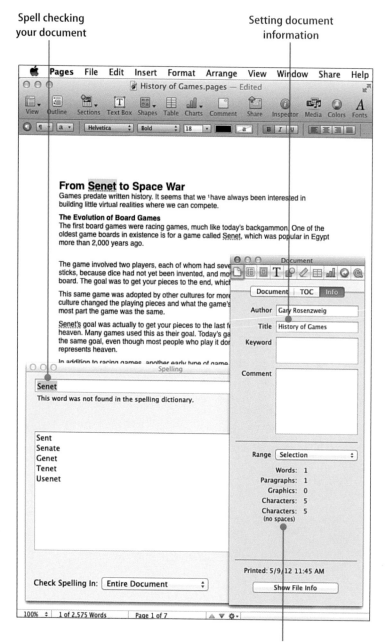

In this chapter, you'll learn how to produce better documents, including:

→ Customizing the toolbar
→ Searching and replacing text
→ Changing view and zoom options
→ Using Auto-Correction
→ Checking spelling
→ Examining document statistics
→ Using the Help menu

Document and Writing Tools

Now that you know how to create almost any kind of document in Pages, how can you create *better* documents? Also, how can you create documents *better*—more efficiently and with fewer errors?

There are a variety of tools in Pages and ways to customize Pages to help you produce better documents.

Customizing the Toolbar

In every chapter, we have used the toolbar to bring up windows and perform actions—but the toolbar can do even more if you let it. By customizing the toolbar, you can add other functions and remove ones you don't use.

1. With any Pages document open, choose View, Customize Toolbar. You can also Control-click or right-click (two-finger click on a trackpad) the toolbar and choose Customize Toolbar.

2. A large dialog will appear over the document window.

3. Drag any icon from the toolbar into the dialog to remove it from the toolbar.

4. Drag any icon from the dialog into the toolbar to add it.

5. Drag the large set of icons to the toolbar to reset the entire toolbar.

6. Drag this Space icon to the toolbar to force a space between icons. This can be used to visually group icons on the toolbar.

7. The Flexible Space icon will create a space that expands as the document window changes size and there is more room on the toolbar.

8. You can choose to show the icon and text on the toolbar, just the icon, or just the text.

9. You can switch between large and small icons.

10. Click Done when you have finished customizing the toolbar.

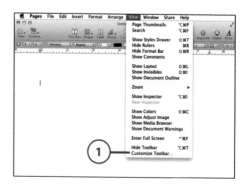

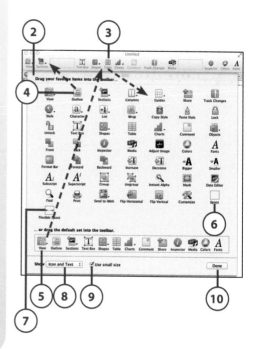

Objects Button

If you keep adding buttons to the toolbar, it gets a little crowded. One button, however, the Objects button, will actually give you more space. It acts as a replacement for the Text Box, Shapes, Table, and Charts button. All four of these elements can be selected by clicking the Objects button. Therefore, add the Objects button to get rid of the other four to free up some space.

Searching and Replacing Text

If you are working on a large document, it is important to be able to search for text. You may also want to search and replace all instances of text in a document.

Simple Search, Sidebar Method

There are actually two ways to search for something in Pages. The first is to use a special search sidebar.

1. Choose Edit, Find, Search.

2. The search sidebar appears. You can choose Edit, Find, Search again to hide it.

3. Type the text you want to search for in the search field.

4. You can see the number of times that phrase has been found.

5. A list shows you each match. Click any item to jump to it.

6. The match is also selected after you click it in the list.

7. Click the magnifying glass icon to reveal a small menu. You can choose whether to match case or whole words. You will also see a list of recent searches.

8. Click the small X to clear the search field.

Search Sidebar Versus Dialog

You may decide you like one of these two search methods and use it exclusively. However, the search sidebar has the advantage of showing you all matches in one list. The dialog is quick to call on with the ⌘-F keyboard shortcut and has extra advanced search options.

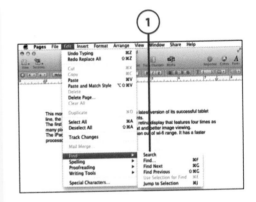

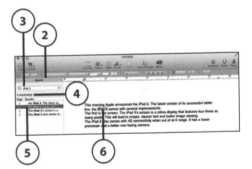

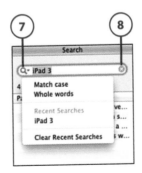

Simple Search, Dialog Box Method

The other type of search involves just a simple dialog.

1. Choose Edit, Find, Find. Alternatively, just press ⌘-F.

2. The Find & Replace dialog appears.

3. Choose the Simple mode for this dialog.

4. Enter your search phrase.

5. Click Next to search for the phase after the current placement of the text cursor. You can continue to click Next to look for more instances.

6. The text is selected in the document.

7. To go backward and look for an occurrence of the phrase before the text cursor, click Previous.

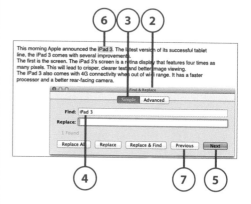

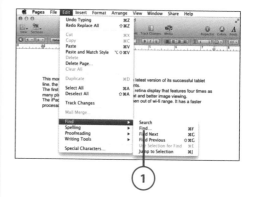

8. Click Advanced to see more search options. In addition to the ability to match case and search only for whole words, like in the search sidebar, you get many other options.

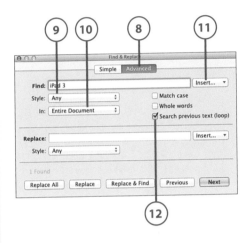

9. Choose the style that the phrase should be found in. This helps you search for text in titles, captions, bullet lists, and other special styles, ignoring body text.

10. Search either the Entire Document, including headers, footers, footnotes, and so on, or choose Main Text Body to omit those items from the search.

11. If you want to search for something with special characters, such as tabs or paragraph breaks, you can insert representatives for those characters with this pull-down menu.

12. With this option checked, your search will loop as you reach the end or beginning of the document by clicking the Next or Previous button.

>>Go Further HANDY KEYBOARD SHORTCUTS

Although the sidebar and dialog are easy to use, learning some keyboard short-cuts can make searching even easier. After you have searched for and found some text, you can close the dialog and then use ⌘-G to find that same text again. You can continue to use ⌘-G to find every instance of the text in your document or add the Shift key to search backward.

Another handy one is ⌘-E. This sets the currently selected text as the search text. Thus, if you see the word *book* in your text, you can select it, press ⌘-E, and then press ⌘-G, and you will be taken to the next instance of the word *book*.

Find & Replace

One advantage of the Find & Replace dialog over the search sidebar is the ability to replace text.

1. Use ⌘-F to bring up the Find & Replace dialog.

2. Enter your search phrase.

3. Enter the text you want to replace it with.

4. Click Next to go to the next occurrence of the text.

5. Click the Replace button to substitute the replacement text for the found text.

6. Using Replace & Find, you can replace the text and move to the next occurrence of the text with one click. You can click Replace & Find multiple times to keep replacing instances of the search phrase.

7. Using Replace All will replace all occurrences of the search text with the replacement text throughout the document.

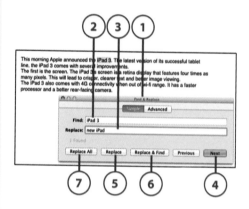

Review, Replace, and Find

The advantage of using Replace & Find as opposed to Replace All is that you can review each substitution. If you want to replace most occurrences of something, but not all (or you are not sure), then Replace & Find lets you see each item before replacing it. You can then choose Next instead of Replace & Find to skip to the next occurrence without replacing it.

Changing Styles for Replacement Text

If you switch from Simple to Advanced mode in the Find & Replace dialog, you can insert special characters and select a style for the replacement text.

Changing View and Zoom Options

While writing, it is often nice to be able to see your words in large, clear text. You have several ways to do this, one of which was pointed out in "Using Full Screen Mode" in Chapter 1, "Working with Word Processing Documents."

But even without using full screen mode, you can still enlarge the text of your document and take advantage of larger screens on some iMacs and MacBook Pros.

1. Click the lower-left section of the bottom bar in your document window.

2. Choose a percentage to scale the entire page. This scaling only affects your viewing as you type and edit. The document remains the same. An amount such as 125% or 150% can make it easier to read and edit your text.

3. You can also scale the text to fit the width of your document window, or the width and height.

4. You can choose Two Up to fit two pages across the width of your document. This is handy if you have a typical wide screen and want to use as much of it as you can while still seeing the entire vertical height of each page.

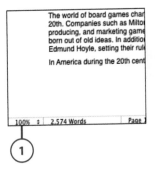

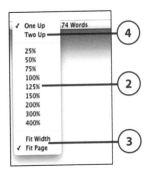

Using Auto-Correction

Pages has a variety of options that will help you avoid mistakes. You can find these in the Pages preferences.

1. Choose Pages, Preferences. Then click Auto-Correction.

2. The Use Smart Quotes option allows you to use the plain quotes key usually found to the left of the Return key. It will substitute the curly quotes in the proper direction according to the context.

3. The Fix Capitalization option automatically capitalizes the first word of a sentence, even if you forget.

4. Superscript Numerical Suffixes will convert the letters *st, nd*, and *rd* after 1st, 2nd, and 3rd, respectively, to smaller superscript letters.

5. Automatically Detect Email and Web Addresses will look for words that are email addresses or URLs and make them hyperlinks.

6. Automatically Detect Lists will start a numbered list automatically if you start lines with "1.", "2.", and so on.

7. Automatically Use Spell Checker Suggestions will substitute words you type if the one you type isn't in the dictionary, and only one possible suggestion is found by the Spell Checker.

8. Symbol and Text Substitution will turn on the option shown in the list below it. This makes automatic substitutions of one set of characters for another.

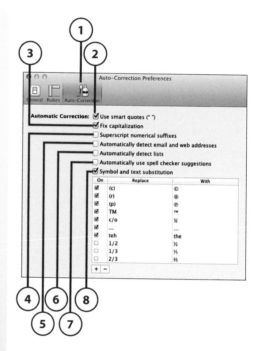

9. In this example, part of Pages' default set, the three characters will be replaced by the copyright symbol. This simply makes it easier to type a symbol like this without needing to go to any special menus or windows.

10. This is an example of one word being substituted for another. Often *teh* is typed by mistake instead of *the*.

11. Click the + button to define your own text substitution.

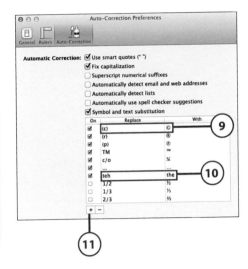

Text Substitutions as Shortcuts

You can define almost anything you want as a text substitution. For instance, if you need to type a long and difficult word often, such as *pharmaceutical*, you could set a substitution for "pharm" to be replaced with "pharmaceutical." You can even set "workadd" to be replaced with your work address, or "sname" to be replaced with your school's name.

Checking Spelling

As you have no doubt already observed, Pages will underline in red any word that it does not recognize. You can turn this option on and off by choosing Edit, Spelling, Check Spelling While Typing.

If you prefer to go through your document and examine potentially misspelled words, one by one, you can do it using one of two methods.

The first is to use Edit, Spelling, Check Spelling (⌘-;). This will advance to the next potentially misspelled word. It will be selected, so you can just type to replace it.

Alternatively, you can use the Spelling window for more functionality.

1. Choose Edit, Spelling, Spelling. This brings up the Spelling window. Or use ⌘-Shift-;.

2. The first potential spelling mistake is selected. You can still simply type to replace it.

3. The word is also shown in the window. You could click in this field and retype the word.

4. You could then press Change to send the change to replace the original word in the document.

5. You could also skip this word and go on to the next.

6. A list of possible suggestions allows you to double-click one to replace the word.

7. You could also click Ignore to skip the word and not come back to it again with this document.

8. Click Learn to add the word to the spelling dictionary so it will never be flagged as a misspelling again in this or any other document. This is handy for names and technical terms that you know you will be using often.

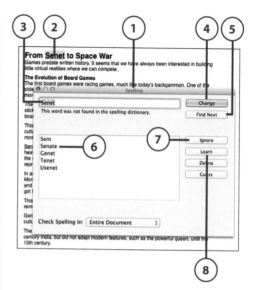

WHAT ABOUT FOREIGN LANGUAGES?

Spell checking uses a specific language. If you look in the Inspector window, using the More section of the Text inspector, you will find a language selection. You can set this to different languages for different sections of text.

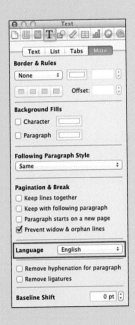

For instance, if your entire document is in English, but you quote a French poem, you can select that poem and change the language to French for that text only. This will allow the spell checker to use the French dictionary for that one piece of text, while using English for the rest.

Proofreading

Proofreading works just like spell checking. Pages will flag problems it detects as you write. You can also step through the problems and view them one by one with Edit, Proofreading, Proofread. And there is also a proofreading window just like the spell checking window.

Proofreading will look for capitalization and punctuation errors, words that can be simplified, improper use of abbreviations, and other things.

1. Choose Edit, Proofreading, Proofreader to bring up the Proofreading window.

2. Click Next to go to the next problem in the document.

3. You can see what text it has identified as a problem here, and even use this field to type a replacement. The text will also be selected in the document.

4. An explanation of what Pages thinks is wrong will appear here.

5. You can double-click suggestions for a quick replacement.

6. If you single-click a suggestion, or type your own, you can use the Correct button to replace the text and move on to the next problem.

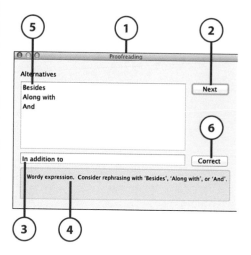

Examining Document Statistics

If you ever need to get some basic information about your document, such as the number of words or paragraphs, you can find it in the Inspector window.

1. Bring up the Inspector window and click the Document inspector.

2. Select Info.

3. You can set an author and title for your document. You can also set keywords and add some comments. All of these fields make it easy to find your document on your Mac using a spotlight file search.

4. If you have some text selected in your document, you can use the Range pull-down menu to switch between statistics for the whole document or just that range.

5. Here you will find various statistics about your document or the selection.

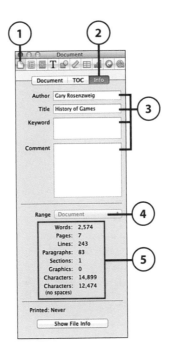

Getting to Statistics

In addition to bringing up the Inspector from the toolbar, you can click the bottom status bar of your document where it reads "X of X Words." Alternatively, you can select some text and then choose Edit, Writing Tools, Show Statistics.

Using the Help Menu

All the way to the right side of the menu bar is the Help menu. As you expect, this is your access to the Pages documentation system. However, you can also use the Help menu to find functions deep inside other menus.

Finding Menu Items

Suppose you can't remember where the Superscript option is in the menu bar. After all, it is several layers deep in the menus. No need to go searching for it. Using the Help menu, you can find it quickly.

1. Click the Help menu.

2. Immediately start typing, and text will appear in the Search field. Just type the first few characters of what you are looking for, such as *super* instead of *superscript*.

3. A list of menu items will appear that in some way matches what you typed.

4. Move your mouse cursor over the suggested menu item.

5. The menu will automatically open up; in this case, the Format, Font, Baseline, Superscript item opens and is selected. A large blue pointer will indicate the menu item. You can quickly move your mouse cursor to this menu item and select it.

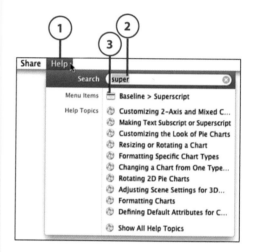

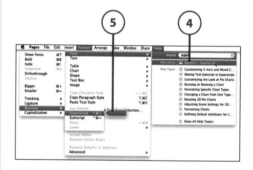

Searching the Documentation

You can also use the Help menu to read more about commands and features.

1. Click the Help menu.

2. Immediately start typing, and text will appear in the field. Suggestions will appear below, although it may take a few seconds.

3. Use your mouse cursor to click a help topic.

4. Text and information about your topic now appears in a new Help Center window.

5. You can use the search field at the top to search for new topics.

6. Click the red button to close the Help Center window.

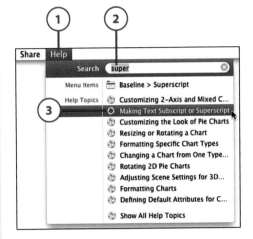

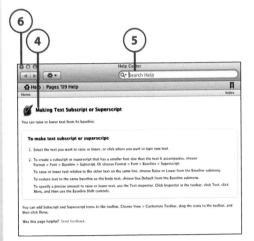

Previewing your printout   Printing options

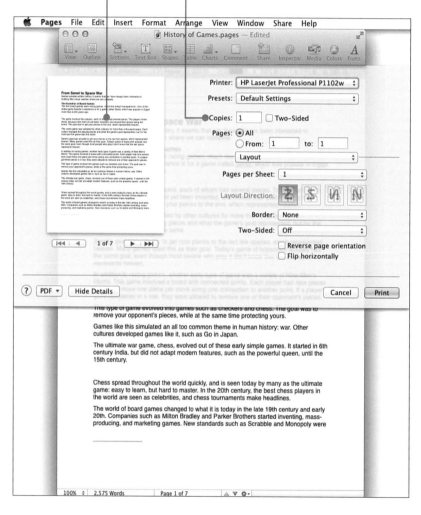

This type of game evolved into games such as checkers and chess. The goal was to remove your opponent's pieces, while at the same time protecting yours.

Games like this simulated an all too common theme in human history: war. Other cultures developed games like it, such as Go in Japan.

The ultimate war game, chess, evolved out of these early simple games. It started in 6th century India, but did not adapt modern features, such as the powerful queen, until the 15th century.

Chess spread throughout the world quickly, and is seen today by many as the ultimate game: easy to learn, but hard to master. In the 20th century, the best chess players in the world are seen as celebrities, and chess tournaments make headlines.

The world of board games changed to what it is today in the late 19th century and early 20th. Companies such as Milton Bradley and Parker Brothers started inventing, mass-producing, and marketing games. New standards such as Scrabble and Monopoly were

_____

In this chapter, you'll learn how to create printed pages from your document, including:

→ Printing your document
→ Setting up the page
→ Exploring print options
→ Previewing your printout

19

Printing

Distributing your document can be done either digitally, which we discuss in the next chapter, or physically on paper. In this chapter, we look at printing your document and what options you have available.

Printing Your Document

1. With your document open, choose File, Print. The keyboard shortcut is ⌘-P.

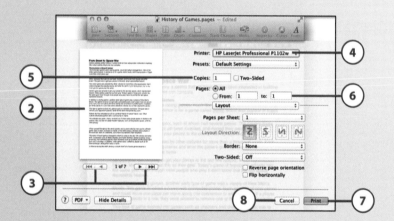

2. The Print dialog appears, along with a preview of what your document will look like on the page.

3. You can use the forward and backward buttons to flip through the pages to check them before printing.

4. If you have more than one printer available, you can select which one to print with here.

5. You can specify the number of copies to print.

6. If you only want to print some, not all, pages of your document, you can set a range here.

7. Click Print to print.

8. If, after previewing your document in steps 2 and 3, you want to edit it some more before printing, you can click Cancel.

CONNECTING PRINTERS

When you buy a new printer, or connect your Mac to a network with a printer you have never used before, you have to add the printer to your system in order for it to appear as a printer in the Print dialog.

This is done in the Print & Scan section of your OS X System Preferences. The list on the left shows available printers, with a green dot next to ones that are ready for use. The + button under that list is how you start the process of adding a new printer.

For many printers, you simply need to follow the instructions that came with the device in order to set it up. Sometimes this means installing special drivers; sometimes it means configuring the printer for your network.

Adjusting Page Setup

In Chapter 5, "Document Formatting and Organization," we looked at document settings and setting page margins. There are more options that change how your document appears on the page, and thus how it prints. You can find these in the Page Setup dialog.

1. Bring up the Page Setup dialog by choosing File, Page Setup.

2. Select the printer you will be using to print this document.

3. Choose the paper size. Lots of standard paper sizes are available, and you can create your own custom size as well.

4. Click here if you plan to print your document in landscape mode instead of portrait. Note that this change will immediately affect your document, changing the page dimensions you see while writing and editing.

5. You can also change the scale of the entire document. This will also immediately change your document as you write and edit it.

6. Click OK to enforce the changes.

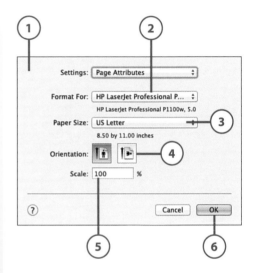

Exploring Printing Options

In the first task for this chapter we looked at simple and quick printing. However, many more options are available in the Print dialog. Let's take a look at some of them.

1. Choose File, Print to bring up the Print dialog.

2. Choose a printer. It is important to note that the options you see in the Print dialog will reflect the printer you have. For instance, in the next step, the Color Matching option would not be present if you are using a black-and-white printer. Some printers have very specialized functions whereas others are very simple.

3. Click the pop-up menu in the middle of the Print dialog to see all of the option categories available for this printer.

4. Choose one of the categories to view the options for that category.

5. Choose the Layout category.

6. You can squeeze more than one document page on a piece of paper. This is useful for printing preview copies of your documents to review.

7. If you are printing more than one document page on a sheet of paper, you may want to decide how those pages are laid out on the paper.

8. You can also choose a border to go around each document page, especially if you are printing more than one per piece of paper.

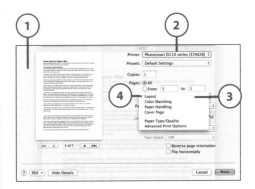

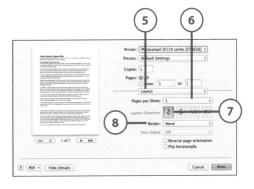

9. Choose the Paper Handling category.

10. You can select only odd or even pages to print. This could come in handy if your printer doesn't support two-sided printing and you want to try to do it by feeding the pages through twice.

11. You can print the document in reverse order.

12. If your document pages do not match the paper size you have in the printer, you can select this check box to automatically scale the pages to fit the paper.

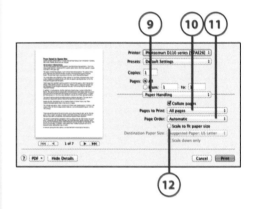

More Print Options

Examine each of the print option categories available to you. Some will be very specific to your printer. For instance, a color inkjet printer should give you options for paper quality and ink use. A laser printer may give you options for print density and quality.

Previewing Your Printout

Although the small preview you get in the Print dialog is useful, you can get a much better preview with a special function included in the Print dialog.

1. With the Print dialog open, click the PDF button.

2. Choose Open PDF in Preview.

3. A temporary PDF file containing your document is created. You'll learn more about creating PDF files in the next chapter. This temporary file is opened in the Preview app.

4. You can zoom in and out as well as page through the document to inspect it.

5. Click the Print button to send the document to the printer through Preview's own print dialog. There should be no difference between printing directly from Pages and printing by choosing Open PDF in Preview and then printing from Preview.

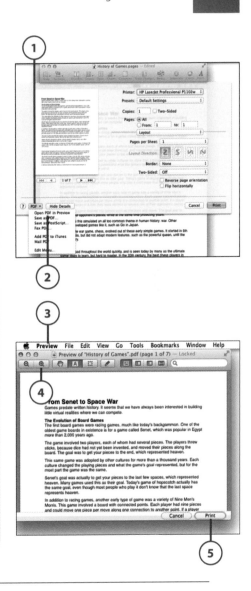

Preview as a Gateway to PDF

While you have the preview of your document open in Preview, you can always choose File, Save to save it. This creates a PDF file that you can then send to others or use to print from another computer that doesn't have Pages.

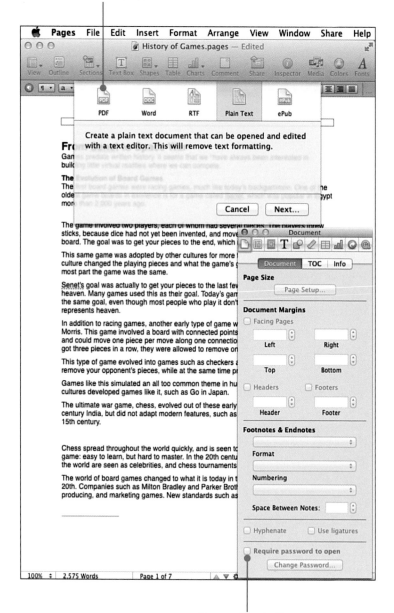

In this chapter, you'll learn how to export your documents into other formats to facilitate sharing with others, including:

→ Exporting as a PDF
→ Exporting for Microsoft Word
→ Exporting as rich or plain text
→ Saving to iCloud
→ Reducing file size
→ Locking and password-protecting your document

20

Sharing and Exporting

It may be more useful and common today to share your documents electronically rather than printing. Pages has a lot of options for exporting documents into formats that other people, even if they do not have Pages, can view.

Exporting as a PDF

The most universally accepted format for reading documents is PDF, or portable document format. Applications exist to read PDFs on Macs, Windows, Linux, iOS, Android, eBook readers, and other mobile devices as well.

1. With a document open, choose File, Export. Alternatively, you can choose Share, Export. Both lead you to the same place.

2. In the Export dialog, click PDF.

3. Choose an image quality. This only matters if you have images in your document and the images are high quality, like photographs. The setting you choose here will determine the amount of compression used on those images.

4. If you like, you can set security options for your document, such as a password needed to open, print, or copy text from a document.

5. Click Next to continue to a normal save file dialog and name the file.

6. Choose a filename for the PDF file. Typically you will want to stick with a .pdf file extension to make sure many different types of computers and devices will recognize the file.

7. Use the various tools in the Save dialog to locate the place where you want to save the file.

8. Click Export to save the file.

PDF for Print Portability

One reason you may want to create a PDF is to allow yourself to print the document from another computer. You can save the PDF and transfer it to another computer that is connected to the printer you want to use. You can then open it and print it using a PDF viewer.

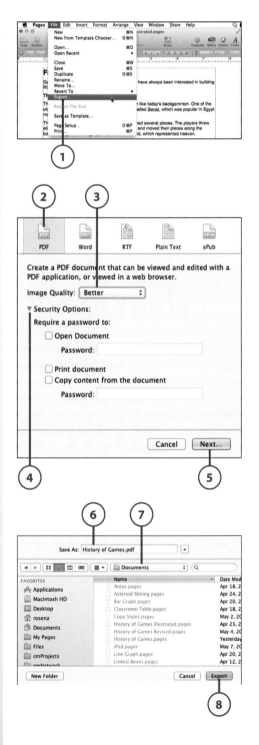

Exporting for Microsoft Word

Pages is only available on Macintosh computers. There is also an iOS version of Pages, but there is no Pages for Windows users. If you are collaborating with a Windows user, you may need to export your Pages document as a Microsoft Word document. Some Mac users may also use the Mac version of Word.

1. With a document open, choose File, Export.

2. Click Word.

3. Click Next to move on to the Save File dialog. Then continue with steps 6, 7, and 8 from the previous task.

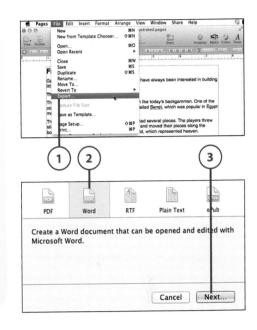

COMPATIBILITY STRATEGY

>>>Go Further

Pages and Word are two different programs. They can both be used to create rich documents featuring tables, charts, and other items, but in slightly different ways. When you export from Pages to Word, sophisticated content may be changed.

So if you know you will be exporting to Word, it is important to experiment early. If you are creating a chart in Pages, then copy and paste that chart into a new document, export it as Word, and see how it looks in Word.

Doing this early, rather than waiting until you are almost done with your document, is a good way to avoid problems.

Exporting as Rich or Plain Text

Exporting as rich text and as plain text are two other ways of making documents that are easily transportable. However, these kinds of documents have fewer bells and whistles than Pages, Word, and PDF documents. Plain text is just text, and even rich text is just text with some formatting.

The process for exporting rich text or plain text documents is exactly the same as exporting PDF or Word documents. You just have to choose a different option in step 2.

However, it is important to understand the difference between these types of files.

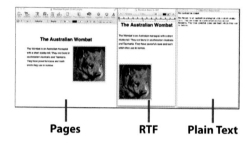

Pages   **RTF**   **Plain Text**

On the left, you can see the Pages document, which has formatted text and an image positioned in a specific location.

The exported RTF file keeps the formatted text. Even the image remains, but the image loses its position. So you can include things such as images in RTF files, but not with specific layouts. It is similar to composing an email message.

The plain text export only includes the text—and the text isn't formatted anymore. The title doesn't appear bold and larger than the rest of the text, and it isn't centered. The font selection is even ignored in favor of whatever font the text viewer uses for plain text.

WHAT ABOUT EPUB?

ePub is another option offered in the Pages export dialog. ePub is used by eBook readers. It is similar to rich text format, in that layout is largely ignored. This is because ePub documents are meant to be adjusted by the user for font size, horizontal versus vertical layout, and so on. Thus, the text is meant to reflow according to the eBook reader and the user's preferences.

If you have composed a document in Pages and find you need to distribute it in ePub format, you can export as ePub. Just be sure to check your results.

If you are interested in creating ePub books, then you might also want to look into Pages' sister app called iBooks Author. It can be used to create eBooks in a special format that can be read in the iBooks app on iPads and other iOS devices.

Reducing File Size

You are usually not thinking about file size when importing photos into a document. However, photos can be large files in themselves, weighing in at several megabytes or more. A document with dozens of photos can easily be hundreds of megabytes in size.

Often you don't need the full high-resolution photos in your document. If your goal is to distribute the document as a PDF file, or even print it from just a standard inkjet printer, you can afford to compress the images some to get a smaller document file while barely making a noticeable change to the quality of the photos.

1. Open a document that has at least one image in it.

2. Choose File, Reduce File Size.

3. You can see how much your document file will shrink.

4. Click Reduce to implement the changes.

You Can Only Compress So Much

If it happens that all the images in your document are already compressed at close to optimal settings, you might get an error message stating that the document size cannot be reduced any further.

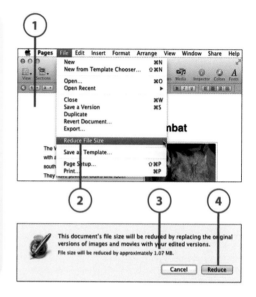

Locking and Password-Protecting Your Document

If your document has secret information in it, or you simply don't want anyone else to be able to edit it, you can set a password.

1. Open a document.

2. Bring up the Inspector window.

3. Go to the Document inspector.

4. Click Document.

5. Check the box next to Require Password to Open.

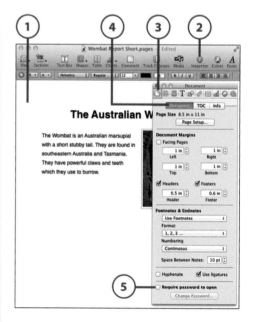

6. Enter a password for the document.

7. Enter the password again as a safety measure.

8. If you can't think of a password, or want to make sure you use a strong and secure random password, click the key to bring up Mac OS X's Password Assistant, which will generate a password for you.

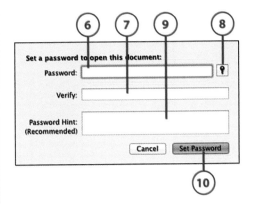

9. You can add a hint to be displayed if the password is forgotten.

10. Click Set Password.

Protect PDFs, Too

The Export dialog for PDFs also enables you to set a password. In fact, you can set two: one for opening, and another for printing. So if you plan to keep the Pages document to yourself and only distribute PDFs, you can leave the Pages document unprotected and protect the PDFs instead.

Index

B

C

My Pages

COVERS Pages for Mac

Learn how to use the Mac's leading word processor and publishing app

Gary Rosenzweig

FREE Online Edition

Safari Books Online

Your purchase of *My Pages* includes access to a free online edition for 45 days through the **Safari Books Online** subscription service. Nearly every Que book is available online through **Safari Books Online**, along with thousands of books and videos from publishers such as Addison-Wesley Professional, Cisco Press, Exam Cram, IBM Press, O'Reilly Media, Prentice Hall, Sams, and VMware Press.

Safari Books Online is a digital library providing searchable, on-demand access to thousands of technology, digital media, and professional development books and videos from leading publishers. With one monthly or yearly subscription price, you get unlimited access to learning tools and information on topics including mobile app and software development, tips and tricks on using your favorite gadgets, networking, project management, graphic design, and much more.

Activate your FREE Online Edition at
informit.com/safarifree

STEP 1: Enter the coupon code: XEMRWBI.

STEP 2: New Safari users, complete the brief registration form. Safari subscribers, just log in.

If you have difficulty registering on Safari or accessing the online edition, please e-mail customer-service@safaribooksonline.com

 Addison Wesley AdobePress ALPHA Cisco Press FT Press IBM Press Microsoft Press New Riders O'REILLY

 Peachpit Press PRENTICE HALL QUE Redbooks SAMS SAS vmware PRESS WILEY wrox